IN GOD'S HANDS

D0582873

IN GOD'S HANDS

THE ARCHBISHOP OF CANTERBURY'S LENT BOOK 2015

DESMOND TUTU

BLOOMSBURY

LONDON • NEW DELHI • NEW YORK • SYDNEY

First published in Great Britain 2014

Copyright © Desmond Tutu, 2014

The Desmond & Leah Tutu Legacy Foundation: www.tutu.org.za

The moral right of the author has been asserted

No part of this book may be used or reproduced in any manner
whatsoever without written permission from the Publisher except in
the case of brief quotations embodied in critical articles or reviews.
Every reasonable effort has been made to trace copyright holders of
material reproduced in this book, but if any have been inadvertently
overlooked the Publisher would be glad to hear from them.

A Continuum book

Bloomsbury Publishing Plc
50 Bedford Square
London WC1B 3DP

www.bloomsbury.com

Bloomsbury is a trademark of Bloomsbury Publishing Plc

Bloomsbury Publishing, London, New Delhi, New York and Sydney

A CIP record for this book is available from the British Library.

ISBN 978-1-4729-0837-7

10 9 8 7 6 5

Typeset by Fakenham Prepress Solutions, Fakenham, Norfolk
NR21 8NN

Printed and bound in Great Britain by CPI Group (UK) Ltd,
Croydon CR0 4YY

MIX
Paper from
responsible sources
FSC
www.fsc.org   FSC® C013604

CONTENTS

FOREWORD BY THE ARCHBISHOP OF CANTERBURY

FOREWORD

This is a very unusual Archbishop's Lent Book. It is written by one of the most extraordinary Christian leaders alive today, or to have lived in the last century or more. Archbishop Desmond Tutu was a crucial figure in the overthrow of a regime of the utmost evil. More than that, he led the way forward into a society that was seeking reconciliation without revenge. He has remained fearless in his public comments, always constant to principle, and never resting on his laurels.

The results of his work, and the work of those alongside whom he struggled, are not complete. Human fallibility means they never can be. Yet a country is emerging whose potential is internationally recognized, and whose hope is in significant part the result of Arch's contribution.

It is easy to see such figures in news reports, to hear their words and wonder what drives them. In this book we see the love for Christ, the generosity of spirit, the immense vision and courage, and the extraordinary virtues which have set the course of Arch's life to date. Just as an x-ray reveals the spine, so here Arch explains his essence, that we may glimpse the framework that has steeled and stayed him through turbulence and trauma. The vision that has emerged out of the profound struggles of his life is one that calls all people to share his hope, regardless of where they come from or what they experience. It is a global vision for a divided and cruel world.

He has written a Lent book in which his own, very distinctive voice is heard clearly. We are drawn in to his story through testimony and narrative; we are drawn in to reflection through comment and humour and passionate declamation. This is a book of transparency about its author. We live the life alongside the author; and the voice we hear, even if we might disagree with some of what he says, challenges us to hear the voice of Christ.

It is hearing – through the voice of Arch – the voice of Christ that gives this Lent book its unique quality and makes it so appropriate. Even for those who already take Lent very seriously, Lent books can become a discipline of some rigour. That is perfectly proper, of course. But beware this book, which may appear deceptively simple – until we allow it to draw us into the great struggle for justice, and become whirled along in the slipstream. As Karl Barth urged, the Christian should have the Bible in one hand and the newspaper in the other (and, as he continued, interpret the newspaper from the Bible, not the other way around). Desmond Tutu compels reflection on both, yet demands continually that we return to the scriptures for the way in which we see the world. Having engaged with the world – in all its injustice and struggle – we are fuelled afresh for the journey with Jesus, not least to the great events of Holy Week and Easter.

In times of conflict we are tempted to react instinctively rather than in obedience to Christ.

Foreword by the Archbishop of Canterbury

This book is different, demanding and dramatic – because it holds us to his call. You will not look back.

+Justin Cantuar
Lambeth Palace
Feast Day of St Bartholomew the Apostle,
24 August 2014

PART ONE

1
THE SUBVERSIVENESS OF THE BIBLE

I must tell you this old story which you probably know. Sometimes it was related by Blacks when they considered their plight as victims of the injustice and inequity of racism. 'Long ago, when the missionaries first came to Africa, we had the land and they had the Bible, and they said, "Let us pray". We dutifully closed our eyes, and at the end they said, "Amen", and when we opened our eyes – Why! the Whites had the land and we had the Bible.'

This is not being fair to the missionaries. They may sometimes have been the vanguard preparing the way for their colonising compatriots, but I want to pay a very warm tribute to most of these Western missionaries. Most of us in the Black community owe our education to those indomitable Europeans who built outstanding educational institutions such as Lovedale, Healdtown, and the University of Fort Hare in the eastern Cape, which served not only South Africa but other countries of the African continent, whose citizens graduated from what was one of the few institutions providing university training for Blacks. Nelson Mandela received nearly all his education in one or other of those institutions.

Many of us would have succumbed to the diseases prevalent in poor and unlettered homes had it not been for the clinics and hospitals that the missionaries erected. It would be to malign some of the most dedicated and selfless human beings that ever walked God's earth. Is the outrage that the story evokes justifiable? Is it the case that what the story tells would have been a bad bargain, losing one's land and all that goes with it in exchange for what? The Bible. Would it have been the case that the missionaries had pulled a fast one over the gullible Blacks? I want to assert as eloquently and as unequivocally as I can that it was not so. We Blacks had in fact not struck a bad bargain. The missionaries placed in the hands of Blacks something that was thoroughly subversive of injustice and oppression.

Before I go on to show how subversive the Bible is of injustice and oppression, may I digress a little? It will be a digression that enhances the wonder of the biblical assertions regarding us human beings. Like the Hebrews, other nations had their own myths; these stories about the beginning times. One of the more well-known is the Babylonian story of the beginning times, Enuma Elish, in which Marduk, after defeating the dragon goddess, Tiamat, reigns supreme.

Two important points emerge that distinguish the biblical account from that of the other peoples such as the Babylonians. In the Babylonian epic, the human being is created in part from the dismembered carcass of Tiamat, the defeated goddess of chaos, so he already has as a constituent part of his makeup something evil from the portion of Tiamat's carcass out of which he is created. More importantly, human beings are created to do all the backbreaking work, to slave so that the gods can have fun and enjoy themselves. It would thus not be surprising for such human creatures to behave badly. They were in a sense programmed to go astray, because of the evil element in their constitution.

The biblical narrative is majestic in its beauty. God is one – although in the Hebrew Bible God's name is a plural form, *Elohim*, the biblical God is transcendentally one; there is no battle of the gods. There is no struggle out of which creation emerges. No, God – the God of the Bible – has but to speak and this creative fiat brings all into being in an orderly fashion. Perhaps using the plural form was the Bible's way of claiming for this one God all the divine power which, in religions like that of the Babylonians, required many gods. God has but to speak: 'Let there be...' and there is.

And, crucially, what comes into existence comes each in its order: the heavens, the separation of the waters to bring the rest of God's creation into being (since the firmament separated the waters above the firmament from those under the firmament), etc. The heavenly bodies, the sun, the moon and the stars are not there to be worshipped or to be feared as having a baneful influence on the fate of humans. You know how, even today, we speak of 'thanking our lucky stars', and many magazines and newspapers run columns about horoscopes and what the stars foretell. It is amazing just how many us of still think that these celestial bodies can influence our fate for good or ill. The biblical account puts them, as it were, properly in their place. They are not gods; no, they are there to serve humankind, to give light by day or by night.

The divine fiat is all powerful. Yes, God has but to speak and all comes into being in orderly fashion. And, after each act of creation, God pronounces the divine stamp of approval – 'And it was good'. We are so used to the words that we do not realize their crucial importance. Many in the ancient world sought, as perhaps we do, to identify the source of evil, of the wrong. Some of the ancient sages found a neat answer by declaring that all matter was evil, whereas all that was spirit was good, both in and of itself. This dualistic view is rejected right at the beginning of our Judaeo-Christian holy book. Otherwise, we would have to condemn our physical selves as inherently evil. There were those who indeed believed that to be so, and either indulged the senses or vigorously denied their physical selves by strict fasts etc.

Had this view prevailed then it would have ruled out the Incarnation, since it would have been impossible for God – all Holy Spirit – to be intimately united to our physical selves, as

13

we believe happened when the Son of God, the second Person of the Trinity, assumed our full humanity. This includes our physical nature, which He did not discard when He rose from the dead and when He ascended into Heaven, where He presented to the Father all His members: those who, through baptism, have been united irrevocably with Him as members of His Body.

So what was being asserted in the first account of creation in the Bible has an absolutely crucial relevance for our Christian faith and for our attitude to God's material creation. And so it is that, after each creative act by divine fiat, God the Creator pronounces the divine approval: 'It was good'. And everything happens in an orderly fashion.

On the sixth day, there are some significant changes. Previously, up to the fifth day of Creation, the divine formula was 'Let there be...', and it was; and then the assertion of divine approval – 'God saw that it was good'. On the sixth day the formula changes, as if to alert us that something quite momentous is about to happen. God does not say: 'Let there be...'. No, God summons the divine council and says: 'Let us create man in our own image and likeness…'. And it was so.

After this momentous act, when man and woman are brought into being out of nothing (*ex nihilo* – just by God's word; and note that it is both man and woman who are so created), the formula expressing God's approval has also changed. It does not say: 'God saw, and it was good'. No, the assertion is categorical and emphatic: 'God saw everything that God had created and it was <u>very</u> good'.

This embraces everything in creation. There have been people who thought, for instance, that sex was not quite holy – or it might be food, or music, or anything that human beings enjoy. They wanted to castigate these as somehow not acceptable, as somehow tainted. If sex was not good, how did they think Adam and Eve (not so named in the first account of creation) would obey God's injunction to be fruitful and multiply? – surely not just by staring into each other's eyes! Everything God has created is good; in fact, it is very good, and there to be properly enjoyed by us.

In God's Hands

And humans were given dominion over all of creation. That is why we were created: to be God's viceroys, to be God's stand-ins. We should love, we should bear rule over the rest of creation as God would. We are meant to be caring in how we deal with the rest of God's creation. God wants everything to flourish.

It gives us a huge responsibility – that we should not ravage and waste the natural resources which God places at our disposal for our wellbeing. We must be caring, to fulfil our mandate as those who bear rule in God's name. This obviously has a great deal to say to us about what we have done and are doing to the environment. Concern about the depletion of the ozone layer, about the emissions of greenhouse gases, about the melting of the ice caps, are not merely political concerns. For us, who hold the Bible to be central to our faith, these are issues that should not be peripheral, or the concern of people who are regarded as a bit peculiar. These are issues that are made central to our lives because the Bible is central to our lives – or should be.

The melting ice raises sea levels and we know that many island homes have been washed away and are no longer available as places for human habitation. Trees are dying because of the rising salt seawater. Grazing is disappearing, becoming more and more scarce, leading to conflict amongst cattle-, sheep- and goat-rearing communities.

God asks us to be co-creators with God, to be those who promote flourishing, not promoting death. We are being warned that it may be that we have only a few years left before the changes we are effecting through our uncaring and ruthless exploitation of natural resources become irreversible. We are, we should remember, God's viceroys, God's stand-ins. We should bear rule as God's representatives. Greed is responsible for our uncaring depletion of fossil fuels, which belch forth the fumes that are destroying the ozone layer. God wanted us to live in a paradise. We are fast falling into a hell of our own making because of our uncaring exploitation.

A few years ago, I attended a service in Tromso in Norway to observe World Environment Day. There was an ice block about five feet tall slowly melting in front of the pulpit, which concentrated my mind as the preacher. The altar party consisted of a woman bishop of the Lutheran Church in Iceland and two young women, one from the Pacific Islands and the other from West Africa.

The Icelandic bishop told how polar bears were drowning because the ice was too thin to carry them and they were drowning in the resultant lakes. She went on to describe how this new development was affecting her own people's lifestyles. They could no longer go skiing because the ice was too thin to support their weight. They could not visit one another as easily as before. The Pacific Islander told of the trees that were dying because of the salt seawater that was flooding her island home. The West African also related her own people's woes. The desertification was playing havoc with the pasturage, which meant that tribes who had lived peacefully side by side were now at daggers drawn as they jostled for the diminishing available pasture.

Now that service I mentioned was a few years ago. The situations described have not got better, since we have not improved our destructive ways to any significant degree. If anything, we have become even more rapacious. We are exploiting for all it is worth the fossil fuels, for instance in the so-called Indian reserves. The First Nations in Canada are asking for the support of concerned and caring people around the world to help stop the construction of a major pipeline that would convey oil from Canada to the USA.

Opposition to such irresponsible policies is not primarily a political matter. It is essentially a religious, a moral, action inspired by what the Bible asserts about each and every one of us – that we are each a God-carrier, a viceroy, a representative of a righteous and caring God who has given us the extraordinary status of those created in God's own image. An old Jewish story relates how the angels and archangels and everyone and everything in all of creation are brought to order by an archangel announcing as he walks in front of a human being: 'Make way for the image of God'. That's how remarkable we are. Now, let us return to the main subject of this chapter.

* * *

The last thing you should give to those whom you want to subjugate, to oppress, is the Bible. It is more revolutionary, more subversive of injustice and oppression than any political manifesto or ideology. How so? The Bible asserts, as we have shown, that each one of us, without exception, is created in the image of God (the *Imago Dei*). Whether you are rich or poor, white or black, educated or illiterate, male or female – each one of us, exhilaratingly, wonderfully, is created in the image of God.

Our worth is intrinsic; it comes, as it were, with the package. All discrimination is based on some attribute or other: race, gender, sexual orientation, being educated or not being educated, being rich or poor. All of the latter are extrinsic attributes – they can be variegated and we would still be human; we are human whatever these may be. What the Bible says categorically, exhilaratingly, is that what endows you and me with worth, indeed infinite worth, is this one fact: that we are created in the image of God. Our worth is something that comes with the package. It is intrinsic and universal. It belongs to all human beings, regardless.

In the Ancient world the Sovereign could not be everywhere at the same time, so an image of the monarch would be set up in different parts of his territory and it was to be reverenced just as the Sovereign himself would be. The king's subjects had to bow or curtsey before the statue as they would before the king himself; thus for the Bible to say we are the image of God is to make a remarkable and utterly subversive assertion.

Much injustice in our world is because people are discriminated against on the basis of some extrinsic, actually biological, attribute. Hence the German Holocaust, when six million Jews and five million others, including homosexuals, were exterminated by the self-claimed 'superior' Aryans. In South Africa, Blacks were subjected to the vicious system of apartheid. We Blacks were – well, human, but not quite as human as our white compatriots. It was quite revealing when you saw public notices that unashamedly declared, 'Natives (Blacks) and dogs not allowed'. The governing class often treated their pet dogs far better than they treated the Blacks they encountered.

If we really believed what we asserted – that each human being without exception is created in the image of God, and so is a God-carrier – then we

would be appalled at any ill-treatment of another
human being, because it is not simply unjust but
also, shockingly, blasphemous. It really is like
spitting in the face of God. That, in fact, is what
the missionaries had brought us: this book that
is more radical, more revolutionary, than any
political manifesto could hope to be.

St Paul tells the Corinthians that each one of
them is a sanctuary, a temple of the Holy Spirit (1
Cor. 6.19). In the Anglo-Catholic tradition, we
genuflect as we reverence the Blessed Sacrament,
having been alerted to its presence by the white
or red lamp burning in front of it or over the
sanctuary. If we truly believed that we are each
a God-carrier and a sanctuary of the Holy Spirit
then we would not just greet each other by shaking
hands, we would bow deeply as Buddhists do, or
genuflect in front of each other: 'The God in me
greets the God in you'.

You and I cannot be indifferent to the injustices
suffered by so many of our sisters and brothers,
children of the same God and Father. Those
others – God-carriers – are created in the image
of God just as we are. We have no choice. We
who believe that we are created in God's image,

we who are God-carriers, cannot be quiet or indifferent when others are treated as if they were another and inferior breed. We have to oppose the injustice. We have no choice. In situations of injustice and oppression, do not introduce the Bible, for, when it is correctly understood, it is always subversive of that injustice and oppression.

As we have observed, most unjust discrimination is based on one or other biological factor, an extrinsic attribute – gender/race/sexual orientation/physical or mental disability. We do not say our shorter daughter is less worthy, less priceless, than her taller sibling. We see immediately how preposterous it would be to judge them on the basis of this extrinsic attribute. Parents of children with, say Down's Syndrome, often in fact lavish even more love and care on the child who has a mental disability than on those who are more 'normal'.

Women are finally coming into their own, having for far too long been discriminated against, simply and solely because of their gender which, like other extrinsic attributes, is not something they have chosen but a gift from God. We have been guilty of gross injustice against women simply because of their gender. For far too long they were regarded as being a lesser breed, responsible in some primitive exegesis for the fall of 'man' – was it not Eve who succumbed first to the allurements of the serpent? I am not quite sure whether the proponents of this view were aware that they were asserting that the woman was so influential that she could persuade her 'superior' mate to follow her example. Surely a superior creature would have rejected her blandishments with the scorn they deserved!

Modern-day adherents to the doctrine of women's inherent inferiority are perhaps not so blatant, preferring to talk about headships. Women have gone about their business showing they could be outstanding Prime Ministers, Presidents of nations, heads of corporations, etc. When we in our Anglican Church in Southern Africa decided to ordain women to the priesthood, we discovered just how far we had impoverished ourselves previously, and we declared that, if someone could be ordained priest, we could find no theological barriers to preventing suitable candidates (men or women) from becoming bishops. Last year, our Church consecrated two women bishops, the first Anglican women bishops on our continent. Now I rejoice that our mother Church, the Church of England, has voted overwhelmingly in favour of women bishops. I suspect they will ask themselves the question we asked ourselves after voting in favour of women being ordained priests: 'Why did we deny ourselves for so long all this enrichment we are now enjoying from the ministry of women?'

Yes, the Bible is subversive in its opposition to injustice, and I pray too that African governments and our Church in other African countries will end the horrendous injustice that the current homophobia has unleashed. It is not only unjust but totally un-Christian to penalize people for something about which they can do nothing. None of us chooses our race, our gender, our sexual orientation. These are extrinsic to who we are: those extraordinary creatures made in the image of our Creator, endowed with an intrinsic worth that nothing can destroy. Imagine what our world would be like if we did regard one another as God-carriers of infinite worth! How could we mistreat, bomb or torture a fellow God-carrier?

You and I are God's viceroys, God's stand-ins. It is something almost impossible to take in. What would happen in our world were we to act appropriately in relation to this remarkable assertion? That horrid neighbour who plays his music out loud, making it difficult for you and your spouse to carry on a decent conversation or to have a reasonably comfortable night's sleep – well yes, he is actually a God-carrier; he is, whether he knows it or not, God's stand-in. Would you be so caustic in your exchanges with him the next morning?

What about that awful man hogging the fast lane on the highway and dawdling? If his true nature as God's stand-in were revealed, would we be so scathing in our shouted comments? We hope of course that God would be less annoying and unthinking; but would our response to him not be more tempered, more understanding (perhaps he had had a bad night, etc.) if the God in him were more visible?

It is because Christianity has a high doctrine of matter, of the world of the physical, that our holiest ceremonies and rituals rely on physical, material, tangible things as indispensable conduits for the most sublime spiritual gifts from God. Referring to this, Archbishop William Temple would say, 'Christianity is the most materialistic of the great religions' – Christianity uses water, oil, bread and wine as the means of conveying God's spiritual gifts. Our all-holy God did not disdain to unite pure spirit, divinity itself, with the most mundane, physical material things.

Our God became a real human being, not a make-believe or half-phantom. Our God could be born, as we are born, of a mother who conceived, was pregnant and who suffered birth-pangs just like every other human mother; who gave birth to a real human baby that cried and gurgled like any and every other baby. He assumed our humanity in all its fullness, with its strengths and its frailties; experienced all that each one of us has experienced; was tempted, not once but throughout His earthly life. Only thus could He become our Saviour.

As the Epistle to the Hebrews puts it, 'He was tempted like us', but with this difference – 'without sin' (Heb. 4.15). There was nothing that constitutes us as human that He did not know from the inside. As the bishops and theologians of the Church were to assert: 'What he did not assume, He did not redeem'.

It is because of all this that politics, economics, how people are housed, what sort of water they drink, how they are treated – all are of concern to those of us who are Christians. We are creatures of flesh and blood. We were saved not by an angel (pure spirit) – no, we were redeemed by a God (pure Spirit) who became a human being (a union of spirit and matter, body and soul), who fed the hungry, who opened the eyes of the blind and the ears of the deaf, who healed the sick, cleansed lepers and forgave sins, and who raised the dead to life again.

For Him, all of these things were signs of His Father's kingdom, and in one of His parables He declared that we would be judged fit for heaven or hell, not by whether or not we prayed or went to church (though not denying the value of these if they led to good works, however mundane) but rather on the basis that 'in as much as you have done these things to the least of my sisters and brothers, you have done them to me'.

And 'these things' were mundane things, material ordinary things: in giving water to the thirsty, or bread to the hungry, you had done it to Him. No wonder Irenaeus could say, somewhat oddly, 'The glory of God is man fully alive'.

Topics for Discussion

- 'You and I are God's viceroys, God's stand-ins. It is something almost impossible to take in.' *In the Ancient world, the Temple in Jerusalem was the only one without a cult statue in the inner sanctum. Why do you think this was? How might the world be changed if we were to recognise our fellow human beings as having been made in the image of God? Can we see God in non-believers/ adherents of other faiths also?*

- 'Christianity is "the most materialistic of the great religions".' *What do you think Archbishop William Temple meant by this? What implications does this have for the relationship between religion and politics?*

2

WE ARE CREATED FOR COMPLEMENTARITY, FOR TOGETHERNESS, FOR FAMILY

The second creation story found in Genesis Chapter 2*f* is sublime in its simplicity, but oh, so profound in the truths it seeks to convey. 'Then the Lord God said, "It is not good that the man should be alone...".' In a sense, Adam was *not* alone. There was the lush vegetation, and then all those animals gambolling among the trees, and all those creatures teeming in the waters. There are those who would dismiss these stories of the beginning times as so much hogwash. After all, has not science shown conclusively that human beings emerged on the scene after a long process of evolution? Someone with such an attitude would really be like the person who, reading Wordsworth's 'Daffodils' –

> I wandered lonely as a cloud
> That floats on high o'er vales and hills,
> When all at once I saw a crowd,

A host, of golden daffodils;
Beside the lake, beneath the trees,
Fluttering and dancing in the breeze.

– went on to ask, 'By the way, which band was playing?', thereby revealing that he had completely missed the point and was someone who did not understand writing that intends to tell not the 'how' of things but the more profound 'why' behind those phenomena.

Each genre is legitimate, but must be known for what it is and so for what it purports to be doing. How impoverished we would be if the only language we had was what described things in flat, unemotive accounts of their derivation and evolution and not the more sublime aspects of their coming into being. Those who have so discussed these biblical narratives of creation are like someone who wants to bake a cake and castigates a geometry textbook that contains only information about triangles and parallelograms and suchlike but nothing about the ingredients for a cake and how to actually bake one. Surely we would counsel them gently, 'You can find that in a recipe book.' The biblical stories about the beginning times are much more akin to poetry than to geology. After all, no one who might have witnessed the beginning survived to tell the tale! If we accept the truth of evolution, no one – certainly no sentient intelligent human being – bore witness to creation. Those stories are splendid imaginative accounts, seeking to convey fundamental theological verities rather than scientific facts. They seek to communicate the profound truths of the 'why' and the 'wherefore' of the entire process.

And so the narrative asserts that God said that it was not good for Adam, the representative man, to be alone. As we observed earlier, one could have retorted, 'Ah, God, but he is not alone – look at the trees and the birds and all those animals in his paradise home.' And that is the point of the story. It is that none of us could ever be human in isolation, in stark solitude. I need other human beings to help me to become human in my turn. I would not know how to speak as a human being except by learning from and imitating other human beings, and I would not know how to think, nor how to walk as a human being. All these are things I am able to do because I have been nurtured by other human beings.

In our part of the world, we have something called *ubuntu* – the essence of being human. We say a person (*umntu*) is a person through other persons. *Ubuntu* is a highly sought-after attribute. A person with *ubuntu* is generous, magnanimous, hospitable, welcoming, affirming of others. The world did see at least one South African who epitomized this attribute. Nelson Mandela in many ways revealed *ubuntu*. When he emerged from 27 years' incarceration, many feared he would be bristling with rage and a lust for revenge against those who had for so long ill-treated his people so cruelly and unjustly. Instead, he came preaching forgiveness and reconciliation, and throughout what was left of his earthly life he exemplified graciousness, magnanimity, concern and caring.

That story in Genesis proclaimed that you and I and all of us are made for togetherness, for complementarity. None of us can be totally self-sufficient; the totally self-sufficient one is in fact sub-human, so we are meant to celebrate the fact that we don't have everything. I don't have all the attributes: I lack in many areas, so that I can know my utter need of *you* and all that you bring. Even the most powerful superpower in the world cannot be totally self-sufficient. God has so designed our world that we have to rely on others to supply our needs, as they in their turn must rely on those others to make up what is lacking in their produce.

There are many glorious moments when we inhabitants of the earth reveal our true character-istics, as members of one family, the human family, God's family. Just note the amazing outpouring of love and concern and generosity such as at the time of the awful tsunamis. There was no lingering to check whether we were related or not – people knew that they were not really blood-relatives in the technical sense, but did it matter? Perhaps deep down we were being made to realize our connectedness.

That connectedness was there on 11 September 2001, when the Twin Towers in New York were destroyed. There was a global outpouring of sympathy and caring for the United States, for Americans. We saw it also in the outrage right round the world at the abduction of the Nigerian schoolgirls by Boko Haram. Many, many people, celebrities included, have stood with placards reading: 'Bring back our girls'. It has been remarkable that, almost without exception, the placards referred to 'our' girls, as if subliminally we were acknowledging our unity as fellow human beings.

St Paul, preaching in the Areopagus in Athens, declares that God created us from a single ancestor (Acts 17.26). He wanted to underline the fact of our belonging to one family, metaphorically speaking. But it may be one of God's little jokes. Not far from my home are caves which have been identified by geologists and those who study these things as the cradle of humankind. After all the fuss about racism and superiority, the divine joke is that we are all Africans! What was all the fuss about? It has been established by the experts that humankind first saw the light of day in Africa, and from there spread out to populate the globe. For those of us who are not African or dark-skinned, might it just be a salutary thing to bear in mind, that those you might have tended to look down on are actually your ancestors? I can imagine how the residents of heaven must sometimes be rolling in the aisles at some of our activities and attitudes, our pomposities.

This doctrine about our essential unity can be even more disconcerting. Why is it that we continue to spend obscene, indeed diabolical, amounts of money, running into trillions of dollars, on what we call 'defence budgets' when, as we very well know, a minute fraction of those budgets would ensure that every single child on earth would have enough to eat, would have clean water to drink, would have a decent home and receive a good education?

In a normal, healthy home we don't say, 'Granny, you will get food equal to the contribution you make to the family budget.' That would be an awful family indeed. A baby contributes absolutely nothing to the family budget and yet, in a happy home, we lavish the baby with dollops of love and attention. In such a family, it really is to each according to their need and from each according to their ability. That is what God hopes will happen as we contemplate our relationships in our global home.

Why can we be so seemingly uncaring that we are unconcerned that our governments spend the amounts they do on, say, nuclear armaments, when we could feed nearly the entire world population with those funds? It is even more incomprehensible because, if a nuclear war were to break out, there would be hardly any survivors, and those who did survive would be left in a devastated radioactive wilderness.

What really is the sense in keeping an arsenal which you hope desperately you will not need to use? What if a mistake happens, when somebody accidentally trips a switch with devastating consequences? Why do we not try to cultivate relationships that remind us all of how we need one another, how we prosper when all prosper? We should not want to be utterly self-sufficient; that just makes us less than human. We are made with inbuilt insufficiency so that we can know our desperate need of the other, of the one who makes up what is lacking in me; *that* is why God could say: 'It is not good for him to be alone'.

I have often been fascinated as I watch a symphony orchestra. There are all those magnificent instruments: the violins, the cellos, the trumpets etc. The composer will have set down music for each of these instruments. Now and again the conductor will point to the back where someone who is holding a triangle will dutifully strike it and produce its 'ping'. Now, in our view, that is perhaps an insignificant instrument and the sound might be one we would not miss, and yet, in the conception of the composer, something irreplaceable, something unique would be lost to the total beauty of that symphony if that 'ping' were not to happen.

Something quite irreplaceable would be lost to the glorious worship of heaven if your or my particular 'ping' were to go missing. Each one of us is utterly unique. There is no one quite like me – not even my identical twin (thank God). I have gifts that you don't, but that is as it should be, so that you may know your need of me to complement you. But, equally and exhilaratingly, you have gifts that I don't, and that is why I exist and why you exist, so that we can make up what is lacking in one another. It is in this sense that God said it was not good for Adam to be alone.

Whenever we celebrate Mother's Day I always try to underline that there would be no Mother's Day without a father, and that in a profound sense Mother's Day is also to be celebrated as Father's Day and vice versa.

What sort of world would evolve if we genuinely and deeply accepted that we were indeed members of one family, the human family, God's family? Would we still be able to sow as much mayhem and destruction as is happening now in Syria, or in South Sudan, or in the Central African Republic, or in the stand-off between North and South Korea? If those schoolgirls were really members of our families in a way that we all acknowledged, would we countenance their abduction in such a cold-blooded fashion by abductors who declare that it is wrong to educate girls and that they will be sold for $12 each?

Would we not have been appalled by such things as the Nazi Holocaust, which exterminated as if they were garbage six million Jews, as well as another five million victims including homosexuals and gypsies? Does Shylock in Shakespeare's *Merchant of Venice* not utter the anguished cry of all who have had their humanity denied because one biological feature has been highlighted as somehow bestowing humanity on its possessor or denigrating one who lacked it?

It is amazing that for so long, and even now, we have been able to denigrate persons created in the image of God because we have decided that a particular attribute bestows 'real' humanness. And so we in South Africa knew what it meant to see those signs: 'Natives and dogs not allowed', or to be denied admission to a university because it had been reserved for Whites only.

Seeking to demonstrate just how utterly ridiculous this latter practice was, I suggested that we should use size of nose as the attribute by which we were to be distinguished. I have a large nose, hence this would be the attribute to seek to possess. How utterly preposterous it would have been if we were to have declared that the entry qualifications to university would not be intellectual ability but that this or that university would be reserved for large noses only! If you had a small nose then you would have to apply to the Minister of Small Nose Affairs for permission to attend the university reserved for large noses.

41

Everyone can see just how utterly preposterous such a policy would be. But no more preposterous than admission policies that used biological external differences to discriminate against others, denying thereby what is so fundamental in the story of Adam and Eve: that it is our differences that demonstrate not the need for separation but precisely the opposite. We were created to be different so that we would realize that we are fundamentally and of set purpose not self-sufficient but that we have an ontological need for the other; that I am created as dependent on others and will remain so, even as I also grow in independence.

We are created for this deliberate network of interdependence, of complementarity, of family – the human family; God's family. Martin Luther King Jr. admonished: 'Unless we learn to live together as brothers (and sisters!), we will perish together as fools.' I have always been struck by the account of Saul's conversion. He was on his way to Damascus to wreak havoc among the Christians when he had the well-known vision which would eventually lead to his conversion, turning Saul – the most zealous and militant persecutor of the young Church – into Paul, the most enthusiastic and theologically brilliant apostle of the faith he had no less enthusiastically persecuted.

Saul had been blinded by the brilliant light that suddenly appeared on the Damascus road. Whilst praying, he had a vision of someone named Ananias coming to lay hands on him and thus restoring his sight. Ananias in his turn had had a vision in which the Lord was instructing him to go where Saul was lodging, and to lay hands on him so that he could recover his sight. Ananias remonstrated with the Lord, quite aghast that he should do anything to help that so-and-so who had come from Jerusalem to wreak havoc with the Lord's followers. The reluctant Ananias was persuaded to go, however, and what I have always found intriguing is the greeting with which Ananias saluted the formerly predatory Saul. Quite amazingly, really staggeringly, Ananias addresses him as 'Brother Saul...' (Acts 9.1–19). Does it not echo the words of our Lord after His resurrection when He said to Mary Magdalene: 'Go and tell my brothers that I am ascending to my Father and their Father...' (John 20.17)? 'My brothers'! when we expected Him to have been outraged saying: 'These so-and-so's...', one of whom had betrayed Him, another had denied Him not once but three times, and all had forsaken Him – yes, those 'brothers'.

That was the last thing I would have expected. But it does seem as if the early Christians believed that they had been initiated into a new fellowship that did turn the accepted order upside down. In such a sharply stratified society with ladies and gentlemen, senators, members of the nobility, worthy citizens of the Roman Empire, free men and slaves, the Church presented a new kind of fellowship. They kissed one another as members of one fellowship which discounted the divisions of their contemporary society. In this fellowship, slaves were the equals of their owners and women had rights denied to them by the secular authorities.

In those early days, Christians went so far as to sell their possessions and share the takings in the common purse. No one, according to the Acts of the Apostles (even if it is a somewhat idealized description), claimed their property or its price as their own (Acts 4.32). It was a way of demonstrating that they were family, and as such they felt constrained not only to share but to do so joyfully. (It may also have been in part that they expected their Lord and Master to return soon, in the so-called *Parousia*, to usher in the final consummation of all things, when God would be all in all.) No wonder the admiring pagans could declare: 'How these Christians love one another!' Then, it was said in praise rather than sarcastically.

Yes, it is not good for Adam or anyone else to be alone. We are made for one another. We are made for togetherness; we are made for complementarity; we are made for family; we are made for the human family – God's family. We are made to inhabit a delicate network of togetherness.

Topics for Discussion

- 'It really is to each according to their need and from each according to their ability.' *If we take this seriously, what are the implications for our tax system? for benefits? for the Welfare State? Is it possible to organize society on an entirely voluntary basis, according to these principles?*

- 'Martin Luther King Jr. admonished, "Unless we learn to live together as brothers (and sisters), we will perish together as fools."' *What does it actually mean to live together as brothers and sisters?*

3
THE BIASED GOD

We have been conditioned to accept that the law of the universe we inhabit is that we are accepted because we deserve it, because we have earned it. Quite early on we learn, because a frustrated, hardworking parent shouts, 'Mummy does not like a naughty boy/girl!', that we are loved because it is a reward for good behaviour. We carry that attitude into life and believe 'everyone for him- or her-self and the devil take the hindmost'.

We are quite bamboozled when we encounter the God of the Bible. The crucial paradigm of our Bible is the story of how God rescued a rabble of slaves, long before they had done anything to deserve to be chosen. They were not even an attractive lot, when God intervened decisively in their history. They were not even a nation. They were a raucous bunch, often at one another's throats, as when Moses had to intervene in a brotherly quarrel; they would have none of it and rejected his attempts at bringing peace between them.

Now there must have been many, far more attractive people, far better organized, a great deal more worthy of being saved than this squabbling lot of Hebrew slaves. And that is the point of the story – they were not smart, or orderly, or friendly. They had nothing positive to commend them, and yet God chose them. Our God is that kind of God, who loves us, not because we deserve it as something we have earned, nor because we are lovable. No, we get to be lovable only *because* God loves us.

And this is a God who intervenes on our behalf, not because we deserve it, but because God's love is given freely. It is grace. It is not earned; it cannot be earned. It does not need to be earned. It is given freely, and that is why God is a God who is not even-handed. No, God – our God, the God of the Bible – is a biased God. And so God acts on behalf of a squabbling bunch of slaves, and thereby leaves us a paradigm about the kind of God that God is. God acts on behalf of those who have no one to take up the cudgels on their behalf; who do not deserve God's action.

We find it very difficult to understand this way of doing things because we have almost been programmed to expect reward for effort. And there is a place for that. We want the best doctor, obviously, when we are unwell. We want the best lawyer when we are involved in litigation. Those are spheres where the conventional effort/reward paradigm is appropriate. But, in the sphere of our relationship with God, it is a totally inappropriate way of approaching things.

And so, when God sees a people suffering, God acts and intervenes on their behalf because God is a biased God, biased in favour of the weak, the oppressed, the downtrodden, and the despised. It is almost correct to say that God cannot help it. God is biased, and what a tremendous joy for those who have suffered in our world, those who have been downtrodden and excluded, or in any way pushed to the margins. God showed, in the story of the Exodus from Egypt, what God's fundamental character is.

As we have seen, it is not as if these slaves were an attractive lot but rather that, when there is need, God can't help stepping in on the side of those who are suffering. Many times, those whom God had first redeemed from bondage thought they had earned the right also to be redeemed from slavery in Egypt. Whenever they fell into the trap of thinking that they owed their favoured lot to their own righteousness and their own adherence to the law – that somehow they had earned their redemption, that it was due to *their* efforts – it was necessary for them to be reminded of the prologue to the Decalogue, which is categorical: 'I am the Lord your God who delivered you from bondage...' (Exod. 20.2). Really there should be a 'therefore' before whatever the people were then bidden to do, or to refrain from doing.

> *Long before you were a people, long before you could obey my law, I, Yahweh, did this for you. I delivered you out of bondage. Why? Because I am that kind of God – a generous, caring, loving and gracious God. And you must then obey my law, in gratitude for what I have done already. You obey my law not in order to curry favour with me, not to persuade me to deliver you out of that bondage. I have already delivered you, and your obedience to the law that I am now giving you is to*

express your gratitude for what I have done freely for you.

Almost always the people were pulled up short. They thought somehow that they could, as it were, bribe God by elaborate religious ritual, by observing strict religious laws and offering elaborate worship. And they were constantly being pulled up short whenever they were confronted by the bias of God and by God's real demands.

They probably thought they just might hoodwink God if they did provide elaborate and perhaps costly ritual. Imagine what we would think if, on the occasion of a glorious celebration of the Eucharist in Canterbury Cathedral, with billows of incense smoke and the Archbishop of Canterbury and other worthies resplendent in their eucharistic robes, an untidy, unkempt man were to interrupt their elaborate ritual and shout vociferously that all of this performance was quite unacceptable to God; that it was an abomination to God; that God abhorred it all. To say the assembled worshippers would all be stunned is to put it very mildly – we would wonder where the security personnel had got to, and what they had been doing to allow such an awful spectacle to occur.

Well, something of the sort did take place in the Jerusalem Temple when, in the middle of some elaborate worship, the prophet Isaiah strolled in and declared that all they were doing was an utter abomination to their God who rejected it all totally, unless it had made them as biased as the God they purported to be worshipping. For God rejected all that ostentatious ritualistic display. What God demanded was that God's people should have God's bias and be concerned for the plight of the widow, the orphan and the alien in their midst. This God was an awkward customer, because this God rejected thoroughly religious observances such as their periodic fasting. On another occasion, the prophet claimed that God wanted their fast to be expressed in feeding the hungry, loosening the bonds of the downtrodden, etc.

Throughout most of the Old Testament, God showed that the nature of God was the same yesterday, today and forever. God had sided with the slaves in Egypt. Now, for instance, when the King of Israel wanted to do something not too outrageous but simply to consolidate the royal property, he offered to buy Naboth's vineyard which impeded that consolidation, or to give him another in exchange. Naboth rejected both offers and King Ahab knew that, in Israel, that was that: he could do nothing further about it except to sulk.

His spouse, the non-Israelite Jezebel, did what she had seen happen so many times in her home country. An awkward customer was snuffed out and that should have been the end of the story, with King Ahab now able to confiscate the dead Naboth's vineyard for free. But not in Israel. God's prophet, Elijah, confronted the king on behalf of a nonentity (Naboth was such a nonentity that his genealogy is not even recorded in the story) and took the king thoroughly to task because God – our God – is that kind of God, always biased in favour of the downtrodden, of the weak, of the despised; a God who is thoroughly biased and not even-handed at all.

It was so even in the case of King David, destined to be the prime ancestor of the Messiah, God's redeemer. Even David could not escape the strictures of the prophet when he sinned, first

by his adultery with Bathsheba but especially
for his murder of Bathsheba's husband, Uriah
the Hittite. The prophet Nathan did not fear
to confront the King, whom he tricked into
condemning himself with a beautiful parable
of the rich man who was loath to entertain his
guests with a lamb taken from his own extensive
flock but instead slaughtered the only animal a
poor man owned. David was so incensed by the
sheer rapacity and injustice of the rich man in the
story that he said the culprit should be executed.
Then he was deeply contrite when Nathan said:
'Thou art the man'.

David accepted his punishment with an amazing
humility – not the way the kings of non-Israelite
nations would have behaved, given their
assumption that they were monarchs of all they
surveyed. The point, though, is that once again
we are shown how the God of the Bible has a bias
in favour of the weak, the downtrodden and the
despised.

The prophets were seething in their condemnation, especially of the ostentatious religious
celebrations which went hand in glove with
a rapacious disregard for the welfare of the

poor, the hungry, the despised, the marginalized; all who were the flotsam and jetsam of their societies. They had no one to speak up for them, and it was God who took up the cudgels on their behalf.

You can imagine the impact of this on people who had been used to being treated like scum. It was almost as if the Bible had been written with our particular struggle against apartheid in mind. And, when the powerful in the land berated us for doing that most awful thing, mixing religion with politics, we used to reply by asking, 'Which Bible do you read?'

We would quote with happy abandon from the books of prophets such as Amos, Jeremiah, Isaiah and others to show that real authentic religion was no exercise in escapism. No, it was earthy and thoroughly relevant to the business of human living, speaking to how we conducted our politics, how we carried out our business trans-actions, how we lived our lives, most especially in relation to the poor and the oppressed. We were those bidden to let our righteousness flow like a river, that we should not sell the poor for a pair of sandals, as Amos had admonished his contemporaries – warning that God was incensed, highly incensed, at such abominable conduct.

When God decided to intervene most decisively in our human affairs, how God did this was highly significant. Again, God did not choose a spectacular way to reveal the nature of God. Clearly, God could have come in blinding splendour and ostentatious majesty, choosing a prominent couple to be the human parents of God's Son. But God chose a subject people as the earthly community of the Son of God. They were very small beer indeed, bowed beneath the grinding yoke of the Roman Empire. His parents were equally insignificant, lacking even the clout to get a room in a crowded inn where the Son of God, King and Creator of the Universe, would be born.

God surely must have intended that we should note the significance of all this. God, in the infant Jesus, was born not in the splendour of an opulent royal palace surrounded by richly attired courtiers. God, the Creator of all that is, to whom all belongs, was born in a stable, nuzzled by cattle and sheep. It was shepherds rather than ladies and gentlemen of the nobility who came to pay their homage. Only the magi from the East, not King Herod, brought the infant Jesus the gifts of incense, gold and myrrh; gifts that have come to be seen as symbolising His divinity, His royal majesty and His coming passion and death.

Most of His contemporaries could not pierce this divine incognito. This nondescript family had to flee from the wrath of King Herod, who feared any potential challengers to his rule, even if they were mere infants; and so the Son of God, the omnipotent One, could know from the inside what it was to be a forlorn and wanted fugitive. He identified with us at the lowest points of our existence, demonstrating in the flesh that this God was one who took sides. This God was not neutral nor, more importantly, on the side of the high and mighty; this God was notoriously biased.

If we had visited Joseph and Mary in Nazareth and had seen Jesus working away in His father Joseph's carpentry shop, there would have been nothing to show that this was not just an ordinary young Galilean learning his father's trade. For of course Jesus did not have the symbol that we take so very much for granted: no, He did not have a halo round His head, as we see in all the religious pictures of Him. We would not have heard someone say: 'Oh, that one – oh, He is the Son of God'.

In fact, as we hear in the scriptures, many were upset with Jesus and by some of the claims He made. When He said to the paralytic, 'Your sins are forgiven. Take up your bed and go home', the Pharisees and the religious leaders took great umbrage at what they considered a serious offence of blasphemy. Only God could forgive sins. We, of course, knowing the whole truth, would have said, 'Yes, only God ultimately can forgive sins – these sins of the paralytic have therefore been forgiven because the Son of God has pronounced them forgiven.' They rejected Jesus because they thought that, when God was made manifest, it would be in spectacular splendour, with all the colours of the rainbow glowing, and blinding light flashing all around. Jesus' opponents often sought to discredit Him by pointing to His pedigree: 'Is this not the son of Joseph and are not his brothers and sisters here with us?'. Clearly they were saying: 'What cheek, who the heck does He think he is?'. Thus it was that they could not recognize a God who came incognito, because God wanted to identify with us even at our lowliest.

You can imagine just what it was like, in the days of our struggle against the vicious awfulness of apartheid in South Africa; how exhilarating it was to assure our people that God was with us, not because we were good and righteous. No, it was all because God – our God – was that kind of God.

When Jesus began His public ministry, after nearly thirty years in obscurity and hiddenness, somehow He patterned His ministry on the history of the people of Israel. He believed Himself to be the Son of God, and the people of Israel also had been identified as the Son of God, especially by the prophet Hosea. Israel had been tempted during the 40-year wandering in the wilderness and the people had failed the test dismally, so that only a very tiny remnant survived this wilderness-wandering to cross the river Jordan into the Promised Land of Canaan under the leadership of Joshua. The true Son of God, this Jesus, was also tempted in the wilderness, for 40 days, representing the 40 years wandering of the old Israel; but Jesus emerged triumphant, after wrestling with the tempter. He went on to the river Jordan to be baptized by John the Baptist, and was filled with the Holy Spirit to help transform God's world, so that it would become what God had intended it to be: a paradise (Matt. 3–4).

In keeping with this typology, when Jesus went forth to re-establish Israel He called 12 men to represent the 12 tribes of the old Israel. It is noteworthy that those whom Jesus chose were not members of the élite of their contemporary society. There was hardly one among the Twelve who could be thought to belong to the cream of the society of His day. Jesus called his disciples mainly from the riffraff, for that was the company He chose to keep.

He upset many in the higher classes because of the dubious company He kept – the outcasts, the despised, the sinners, the marginalized, the prostitutes and even the tax collectors, who were considered to be traitors since they collected the taxes for the much-hated Roman colonial overlords. Jesus did not choose to mix with the wealthy, or the ecclesiastical leaders; his friends included, unusually for the time, womenfolk, some of very dubious character. He was taking a stand against the contemporary denigration of women. Far from flinching when one of these women anointed Him with expensive, perfumed ointment at a dinner in the home of a leading Pharisee, he commended her publicly, which was also highly unusual. His own circle of disciples was quite taken aback to find Him engaged in a deep conversation with a Samaritan woman at the well where they had left Him. This broke two taboos: talking to an unaccompanied woman in public, and moreover to one who was a Samaritan, a race with whom the Jews had no truck. In all these ways, Jesus was again revealing the nature of the God He represented: the God who took sides; who was biased in favour of the powerless, the despised and the oppressed. He saw Himself as having been sent on a mission to seek His Father's lost ones. He told the parable of the Prodigal Son, demonstrating a divine love that waited longingly for the lost one. When the father saw, there in the distance, the figure of the lost one returning, he forgot everything about his dignity but lifted his skirts, doing the unthinkable – revealing his ankles – and rushing helter-skelter to embrace his lost son. He ignored his son's confession, embracing this smelly one wearing tattered and torn rags, and putting a ring on his finger to affirm the family connection, and having him clothed with a rich garment and having the best calf slaughtered in celebration.

The way their father lavished all this on his wayward younger brother incensed the older, well-behaved son. He remonstrated with his father, who in turn responded that his well-behaved son already owned everything that his father had. They had to celebrate in that fashion because the younger son, who had been lost and now was found, was like one who had died and was alive again. Jesus was saying that the divine love is poured out lavishly as a free gift, especially for the outcast, for in a real sense God's joy would be incomplete if they were abandoned.

The parable of the lost sheep underscored these teachings even more dramatically. We have unfortunately been badly misled by the conventional pictures of the Good Shepherd. Most frequently, these pictures depict Jesus as the Good Shepherd carrying a nice fluffy little lamb. Fluffy little lambs hardly ever stray from their mummies. The sheep that is likely to stray is that obstreperous old ram which breaks through a wire fence and gets its fleece torn, and maybe it smells to high heaven since it will have fallen into a ditch of dirty water.

It is no lovely lamb that the Good Shepherd seeks and finds. No, it is this awful, troublesome creature and the Good Shepherd is prepared to leave 99 perfectly well-behaved sheep to go and find not a fluffy little lamb but that awful troublesome old ram. He lifts this smelly old so-and-so – and yes, that is the one He carries on His shoulder and, when He reaches home with this awkward load, He does not shove it into a corner. No, He throws a party for this lost one.

And the punch-line of the story? Jesus says: 'There is greater (not just great but greater) joy in heaven over one sinner who repents than over 99 needing no repentance.' God is in the business of saving sinners because God is that kind of God: a biased God, a God who is prejudiced in favour of sinners.

Topics for Discussion

- 'When there is need, God can't help stepping in on the side of those who are suffering...' *How do we reconcile this with the secular view that it is the suffering in the world which most challenges the idea of God?*

- 'David was so incensed by the sheer rapacity and injustice of the rich man in the story that he said the culprit should be executed. Then he was deeply contrite when Nathan said, "Thou art the man."' *Have there been times in your own life when you have only become aware of your own shortcomings through your reaction to the same behaviours in other people?*

4
You Are Loved

Many, if not most, of us have been inveigled into believing that we had to impress God in order for God to love us. Perhaps, as I have indicated earlier, we, as it were, took it in with our mother's milk. We may have heard our parents in exasperation mutter or perhaps shout that 'Mummy doesn't like a naughty boy/girl', and so we thought we were expected to earn our parents' approval, love, caring, by being in our turn exemplary and well-behaved.

Mercifully, there aren't too many parents who convey that understanding of their love and admiration for their offspring. Yet it does happen. We work ourselves into a frazzle, in order to be considered admirable and worthy of approbation and love. Of course, as we've already seen, there are many situations in our lives where it is perfectly appropriate to demand the best, which then wins our approbation. When we are ill, or when one of our loved ones is incapacitated, we would be silly in the extreme to say that we would be satisfied with the attentions of any old quack. No, we want the best available physician, who did brilliantly at medical school. We are not going to be satisfied to have our loved one treated by someone who barely made the grade. Equally, when we are involved in litigation, we look for the best lawyer around, as was the case when I was General Secretary of the South African Council of Churches (SACC). We were constantly being harassed by the apartheid authority and subjected to the most scurrilous attacks by their propaganda arm, which used the public broadcaster, the South African Broadcasting Corporation (SABC) to mount vicious attacks on the SACC and its staff. Eventually the government appointed the Eloff Commission to investigate us, intending to have the SACC declared what was called an 'affected organization', which as such was forbidden to receive overseas funding. The apartheid government knew that, since we received the bulk of our funds from our overseas sisters and brothers, this would have almost certainly forced us to shut up shop.

The South African government was annoyed that we provided legal fees for those charged with political offences. We supported the families of political prisoners and of banned persons. We provided transportation to, and accommodation in, Cape Town, for families – like Nelson Mandela's family – visiting their loved ones who were incarcerated on Robben Island.

Faced with such a serious situation, we would have been quite comprehensively unrealistic and really stupid to say we would just rely on God's love. No, we needed outstanding human talent to help us act as we believed God wanted us to so we found the best legal team possible, led by a formidable legal mind in (Sir) Sidney Kentridge. He was brilliant, and the upshot was that the government had to abandon their nefarious scheme.

Yes, there are spheres when ability is an important, indeed, crucial, criterion. But, in the matter of our relation to God, it is totally inappropriate. God does not love us because we are lovable. We have said that before and we will repeat it *ad infinitum*: God loved us even before we were created.

Jeremiah did not want to be a prophet. Perhaps he had seen just what a demanding, lonely and painful vocation it was. Prophets tended to be ostracized in their communities, because they pronounced messages that the leaders of their people and perhaps many others in their communities did not want to hear. They were often scathing in their condemnation of their own communities, who fell so tragically short of the high standards that their God expected and demanded.

We saw earlier how Elijah castigated the King, Ahab, and his colluding spouse, Jezebel, when they confiscated Naboth's vineyard; or Isaiah dismissing Israel's elaborate ritual worship as utterly abominable and unacceptable, saying that God wanted a worship that inspired the worshippers to care for the widow, the orphan and the alien in their midst – a threefold class of those who were most likely to be the neediest in any society; or Amos, pouring scorn on his people for their gaudy worship, when they sold the poor for a pair of shoes. He exhorted them instead to let righteousness flow 'like a river' in their communities.

This was not the kind of message that was designed to win friends and influence people for those who conveyed it. So one can very well understand Jeremiah's reluctance to join the ranks of the spokespersons of Yahweh. In the face of such resistance and reluctance, God utters quite extraordinary and in many ways unexpected words. They are words that just knock you over when you consider their implications. God says to Jeremiah: 'Before I formed you in the womb, I knew you ...'. I have often gone on to say, as we considered the import of these words, that God did not seem to know much about human biology. How could anyone know someone even before they were conceived? But that is the point. God is saying to Jeremiah: 'Hey, man, I did not observe that the Israelites were in trouble and start scratching my head in puzzlement and wondering, "Oh dear, they are in a real pickle. What in the name of everything that is good can I do about it?".' And then God would continue: 'Ah, yes! I know what I will do – I will call Jeremiah to be a prophet to deal with this serious predicament in which my people find themselves.' No, that's not how God operated. And it is absolutely stunning what God does in fact do. God says to Jeremiah: 'Even before you were an idea in anyone's head, let alone already in existence; even before you were conceived, *I knew you.*'

That is quite breathtaking: that Jeremiah was no afterthought, no accident. And this breathtaking fact applies to each and every one of us – before we were conceived, God knew that there was going to be a you and a you and YOU.

None of us has come into being as an accident. Some of us might look like accidents, but none actually is. And our worth is intrinsic: God loved us before we were born, before we could do anything to deserve that divine love. St Julian of Norwich says God did not *begin* to love us; God's love for us is as eternal as God is eternal. We do not need to do anything to try to curry favour with God. Can we imagine that? I have been loved *from all eternity*. I am loved now, unreservedly, and God will love me unto the ages of ages. God does not change, so God's love for me, for you, is unchanging and unchangeable.

Especially during the awful days of our struggle against apartheid, I used to say to our people, particularly to the black people who were the victims of that vicious policy, 'There are those who are called VIPs, Very Important Persons. But you are a VSP, a Very Special Person' – and

I would make the crowds wave their arms in the air, exhilaratingly, and shout in unison: 'I am a VSP – I AM A VERY SPECIAL PERSON!!!' and that status was not anything for which we had struggled. It was not something we earned. It was a pure gift from God.

None of us is a copy of another. We are each unique, and each one of us is of immense worth, of infinite worth; a worth that no one could compute.

The story of Jeremiah's call is to be found in the Old Testament. Is there anything in the New Testament that echoes the Old Testament in making this remarkable claim about us? Right at the beginning of the Epistle to the Ephesians (which is attributed to St Paul, though many scholars think he did not write it), the author makes an assertion that echoes that incredible claim found in Jeremiah: 'God chose us in Christ before the foundation of the world'.

Many of us have thought that we had to impress God in order for God to love us, in order for God to accept us. We have thought that we needed to achieve our acceptance by God through our own efforts – to impress God that we were deserving of His divine love and approval. We seem to think that God is somehow hostile to us, setting impossible standards for us to attain before we can hope to be accepted into the heaven of a God who has those impossible standards.

Well, the Scriptures shout a vociferous 'NO' to that view. No, we do NOT have to impress God; to make a God who is basically hostile to God's own human creatures change His opinion of us; to work ourselves into a frazzle to persuade God to accept us, perhaps somewhat reluctantly. No, says the Old Testament emphatically; No, says Jesus, equally emphatically; No, says the New Testament just as emphatically. God loved us even *before* we were, God loves us *now* and God will *continue* to love us unto the ages of ages, for all eternity. This love, this acceptance is *not* based on merit or achievement on our part. No, it is a love that is prevenient: a love that goes before, that precedes *any* achievement or effort on our part. How could I do anything before I existed? Clearly it is preposterous to posit such a view. 'Before the foundation of the world', proclaims the Epistle to the Ephesians. If that be so, if we accept that assertion, then it must be as clear as anything that God's love for me, God's acceptance of me, is sheer gift.

Earlier, I referred to Julian of Norwich who, in her *Revelations of Divine Love*, describes the visions she was granted of God and the ways of God. Almost all of us are familiar with her best-known vision in which she describes holding in her palm something like a hazelnut which, she is told, symbolizes all that was created. When she is perturbed, worrying that all that has been created is so vulnerable that it could disintegrate into nothing at any moment, she is told that it was love that brought it into being, that it is love that upholds and maintains it in being, and that it was brought into being *because* God loved it. Later, she describes another vision where she is deeply puzzled because she sees nowhere that God blames us. And she cannot reconcile what appear to be clearly contradictory truths: the incontrovertible fact that we are sinners, and what has been revealed to her – that God does not blame us, and that nowhere is God wrathful, or taking us to task for our sins. She is reassured that she will one day see the truth that 'All shall be well and all shall be well and all manner of thing shall be well'.

We are incredibly precious creatures. God created us, not because God *needed* us, but wonderfully, exhilaratingly, God created us because God *wanted* us. It is so important for us to bear in mind that God was, and is, fullness of being, pulsating love from eternity to eternity. God needed nothing, God needs nothing, outside of God, to be this pleroma; this fullness of love and fullness of being.

We Christians believe that God is a glorious Trinity, in which the Father pours out the fullness of the Father's being to the Son, who is co-equal and co-eternal with the Father and so can return in equal measure, from all eternity to all eternity, the Father's love and being; and this pulsating interchange of love and being is God the Holy Spirit. How fantastic! So this God who needed nothing, who needs nothing outside the Godhead to be truly God, yet out of *sheer* grace wants us.

What an exhilarating truth – and what a world lies between 'wanting' and 'needing'. We do not say, 'I want oxygen', as if it were a matter of indifference. No, we don't 'want' oxygen; we 'need' oxygen. There is a huge world of difference there. We are endowed with remarkable worth. You and

I have been brought into being by a God who did not need us, who does not need us. We have been created wonderfully because God wanted us, God wants us. We are creatures of love, a love we could not earn, no matter how hard we tried – until we were blue in the face – because *we were not there*. But there is no need for us to strain, no need to try to impress God into loving us, for *God chose us in Christ before the foundation of the world*.

It is a stupendous reality that we do not need to impress God into loving us. God so loved the world that God gave, to us and to the whole of God's creation, the greatest gift that God could give: not this or that thing, but nothing less than God-self in God's greatest gift – God's Son.

God emulated Abraham, who was prepared to sacrifice his son Isaac but had not in fact done so. God offered us God's Son, not just on the cross but in the entire business of the Incarnation. Jesus, the Son of God, did not cling to his status as divine. No, He emptied Himself, divested Himself of the glory and privilege of His divinity, and took on the form of a slave (with all the weakness, and all the humiliation and indignity of a slave), and was obedient, even up to being done to death on the Cross by His own creatures.

This One, who could have called on myriads of angels had He wanted to do so, who could have commanded the forces of nature (after all, He commanded the winds to abate and the waves of a stormy lake to be still), did not use His divine power to escape the consequences of having sided with the poor, the downtrodden, the despised, the ostracized, the sinners in a world such as ours. He did all these things, He suffered the many indignities of His Passion and death on the cross, all to demonstrate the deep love He had for us; to prove that He loved us, not because we were lovable, but rather that we were lovable precisely and only because He had loved us in the past, He loved us now in the present, and He would continue to love us into eternity.

God had always loved us. That is why, in His earthly life, Jesus did not keep company with the respectable, the powerful, etc. No, in keeping with the manner in which He became Man – when He chose to be born of a virgin who was of no status (as neither was her spouse)

– He companied with the riff-raff, the poor, the despised, the insignificant, and He was criticized for the company he kept. We might say, really, that anyone and everyone could enter the heaven of this Jesus; the standards were low and the judge was hopelessly biased in favour of sinners, the weak and the despised. Really, anyone could enter the heaven of this Jesus.

And, as we have seen, this was a God who was ready to leave 99 perfectly well-behaved sheep to go after the recalcitrant and troublesome one, and could then announce that there was not just great joy but *greater* joy in heaven over this obstreperous one, who had caused so much trouble, than over the 99 who needed no repentance. Our God really is amazing.

In Romans 5, St Paul says: 'Whilst we were yet sinners, Christ died for us.' St Paul is, as we should be, bowled over by such an extravagant and generous love. He has meditated on this mystery, for he goes on to say that it is a very rare and unlikely thing to die for another, though perhaps one might consider dying for a good person. But to die for a malefactor, for someone who is not good? No, that is wholly improbable.

And yet that is precisely what has happened in the case of our redemption. It was whilst we were at our worst, at our most unattractive, at our most repulsive – *that* is when this All-Holy One decided to shed His blood for us.

Had Christ waited until we deserved to be died for, He would have had to wait until the cows came home. That is the wonder and the splendour of the divine generosity, of the divine self-emptying (*kenosis*). But it is very much in line with the nature of the God as revealed in the parable of the lost sheep. We have already described the amazing wonder of God's love as depicted in that parable. I doubt that most prudent shepherds would leave 99 sheep by themselves to go into dangerous terrain to search for only one sheep, and that one that must always have been wayward and troublesome. Sheep do not usually stray from their flock just like that. So the lost sheep must have been an exceedingly troublesome old rogue and many shepherds would probably have sighed with relief that that one had disappeared and said with considerable relief, 'Good riddance to bad rubbish.' But the Good Shepherd refuses to give up on this recalcitrant one. The divine love gives up on no one.

For God, there is no one who has a first-class ticket to hell. God, our God, invests all of the divine love and concern in each one of us. God gives to each of us not a piece of love, a bit of God – no, God is never distracted in God's attention. God gives God's all, at every single moment, to each single one of us; to the good and the bad and the indifferent. God loves you and God loves me as if we each were the only creatures God had ever created. It is breathtaking stuff.

If it could be computed, God gives much more of the divine caring and attention to the one on whom the world has given up, the one who is utterly lost. That is how we would interpret the parable of the lost sheep: that God is seemingly willing to risk losing the 99 good sheep just in order to recover the one awkward, troublesome stray. God seems to be saying that something totally irreplaceable would be missing from the joy and beauty of heaven if that lost one were not to be recovered.

My favourite theologian of the Early Church is Origen, who was thought to be less than orthodox because he cut himself to become a eunuch. I admire him especially for his doctrine of universalism. He taught that the divine love is so appealing, so attractive and so irresistible that, in the end, even the Devil will be unable to resist it, and so even the Devil and his demon angels will be drawn back into the heaven of the God of love, when God will truly be All in All.

That is how evil will be destroyed; not by recalcitrants and miscreants being thrown into flames that will burn forever. I find it abhorrent to think that, in the heaven of a God of love, the redeemed would be gloating as they witnessed the damned wallowing in anguish and agony. I don't think I would like to go to such a heaven. I believe that God longs for all the persons God created to enter heaven; to be caught up in the endless worship and adoration of a God of all-consuming love and compassion.

Since God is infinite love, goodness, mercy, wisdom and truth, there will never come a moment when (speaking, as we have to, in spatiotemporal terms) any of God's finite creatures would be able to say, 'Ah, now I comprehend God fully', for then they would not be creatures but would have been metamorphosed into God.

80

God will forever be God, all-loving, all-holy, all-compassionate, and we will grow in our knowledge of God, discovering ever greater depths to that love and compassion and goodness; and God's love will not let God rest until all of God's creatures have been drawn into the ambit of that love and compassion and caring. That is why God would give God's all – God's Son – to win us back home, even whilst we were yet sinners. That is how highly God regards us, how deeply God loves us; and it is all beyond our computing, beyond our comprehension.

God hopes that we, who have experienced the wonder and depth of God's love, will be enlisted in God's team, to seek to draw in those outside, by emulating God's ways. We are enlisted to attract the recalcitrant, ultimately by love, by compassion and by caring. After all, many in the Ancient world were drawn into the Church when they witnessed just how these Christians loved one another.

God, bless us, inspire us, and enable us to draw others to you by our love so that, as the hymn puts it: 'They will know we are Christians by our love'.

We are enabled to love at all only because He first loved us, and was ready to give His all for us – not just when we were good, but especially when we were utterly undeserving of that divine love. *Whilst we were yet sinners, Christ died for us* – this one who chose us to be His, before the foundation of the world. It is mind-blowing. You are someone of infinite worth, because God the Infinite, the Immortal, the all-Holy One, chose you, chose me, chose us all to be His, from all eternity unto the ages of ages. Amen.

Topics for Discussion

- 'St Julian of Norwich says God did not begin to love us; God's love for us is as eternal as God is eternal. We do not need to do anything to try to curry favour with God. Can we imagine that? I have been loved from all eternity. I am loved now, unreservedly, and God will love me unto the ages of ages.' *If God's love is unconditional and everlasting, why should we bother to behave as we believe God wants us to? What are the implications of this for the way we behave towards others?*

- 'Later, she describes another vision where she is deeply puzzled because she sees nowhere that God blames us. And she cannot reconcile what appear to be clearly contradictory truths: the incontrovertible fact that we are sinners, and what has been revealed to her – that God does not blame us, and that nowhere is God wrathful, or taking us to task for our sins.' *What might God blame us for? How does God respond to our sins?*

5
IT'S ALL OF GRACE

In our world, we expect success only as a result of hard work. That is as it should be and that is how people are encouraged and inspired to be conscientious and hardworking. When we go to school, those who excel will have done so almost certainly because they have worked hard, they have studied conscientiously, they have handed in their assignments timeously and they have taken seriously the comments and recommendations of their teachers about which books to consult and what further experiments they should perform. Now, at the end of the term, they will have reaped the fruits of that hard slogging. They will receive the accolades due to them.

Our world is organized on the basis of this work ethic – you reap what you sow. You get the kudos you have earned and, therefore, deserve. This attitude, this manner of doing things, is thoroughly appropriate. As I pointed out in an earlier chapter, this is the so-called work ethic, where you receive rewards in proportion to the effort you have invested in the particular enterprise.

If you are a lawyer, you want to outperform your contemporaries and to reap the rewards of having done so. If, more often than not, you litigate successfully, if you win more cases than you lose, then you will see the benefits in the size of your bank balance. But not only that: you are likely to gain the attention of your peers and you end up being promoted and appointed a QC or its equivalent.

And you will have the chance of honing your skills even further because success generates more success, since the more successful you are, the more briefs you are likely to attract.

And our world can be vicious. The world loves successful persons and is quite cruel to those regarded as failures. This is the success ethic of our world. It is a highly competitive world of dog-eat-dog, everyone for him/herself and the devil take the hindmost. The result is that people boast of how they do not remember when they last had a holiday. In such an environment, stomach ulcers become status symbols as they are signs of just how hard one is working.

When I first came to England in 1962, I happened to attend a garden party. I don't remember why, but we were expected to pay for our own tea and I offered to pay for an English acquaintance whom I had met for the first time at the party. Now he could have said, 'No, thank you', and I would have been perhaps a little miffed, but you could have knocked me down with a feather when he said, 'No thank you – I won't be subsidized'. Wow! But in many ways he was giving expression to the view of many, that they can jolly well make their own way and don't need any help, which might somehow emasculate them (that is, if they are men – and I don't know the equivalent term for women!). So most of us have been nurtured on such fare – work hard to make it, in a harsh and demanding world. Otherwise you have had it. We introduce our children at an early age to this ethos. When they go to school, we want them not only to excel but, figuratively speaking, to wipe the floor with the opposition in intellectual and sporting endeavours. We so order things that, from an early age, our children reckon their worth is not innate, is not intrinsic, or something that comes with the package, but is something that we can earn and, since it is extrinsic, can improve. It is determined by external attributes.

If we have been brought up in an environment that values achievement at any cost, over and above the worth of simply being human, we find it extremely difficult to be comfortable with the ethos of grace – of sheer gift. It must certainly be very difficult for those who have never lacked for anything, who have not quite known what it is to be without, then to experience the exhilaration of being given – of being offered a gift. I do appreciate that it is important that people must not be turned into spongers, who rely on handouts, but this steely attitude that is so suspicious of gifts does make us actually somewhat hard and unattractive, intimidating others from being humane and caring.

I accept that it must be enormously difficult to be open to receiving when one seems to lack for nothing, and that is perhaps why so many who come from affluent societies do not easily understand the wonder of grace, freely bestowed by a deeply generous God. It is of the very nature of

God to give; God would not be God without God's kenosis or self-emptying. That is how God is God, and how God is love: a love tantamount to generous, complete self-giving.

The mother gives birth to her baby having, from conception, continuously given and given to the foetus. The foetus would not be able to develop without the nourishment it receives from its mother. Every mother is like the proverbial pelican, which was thought to feed its young with its own blood (and so was often used to depict our Lord who nourishes us with His precious Blood).

The life of the Godhead is dynamic and alive, for ever and ever. You and I have no real experience of an existence outside (that too is spatial) time and space. We are spatiotemporally conditioned creatures, existing in time and space, with a beginning and an end. God exists outside time and space, so we could not appropriately apply such terms as 'beginning' and 'ending' to God. We do so only in a very transferred sense, because we would otherwise not be able to say anything of any significance about God.

When we speak about God, we use human language only in a very figurative, extended sense. We know that it does not describe this divine reality either fully or accurately, but it is the only language we have. So we can say, 'God is Father' as a generative source of life and existence, but we know that God is not a father in the sense in which a human father is father. If, however, we have no other language and we need to speak about God, and we need to communicate with God, then we can and will do so only with that which we have.

St Thomas Aquinas helped us to articulate much about God but was then vouchsafed a vision of heaven and of God, from which moment he ceased writing about God. St Paul also describes visions he had been vouchsafed, and he declared that he had seen things about which humans cannot speak. Yes, our language is utterly inadequate, but that is the only language we have.

God has deigned to reveal who God is in a manner that we can comprehend, so we have used a plethora of images, each to some extent helping us to catch a glimpse of the blinding glory that is God. Recall the dream of Gerontius, in which he

longs desperately to be brought into the divine
presence but, when his wish is granted, he cries out
in extreme anguish 'Take me away!', for we sinners
cannot bear the splendour and glory of God. It
is too much for our senses; for us, who are to a
greater or lesser extent sinners, it is as if, after being
in the dark, we were to be brought into blinding,
dazzling sunshine. Our systems cannot tolerate it.
Sinners cannot bear the wonder and splendour of
God's glory. That is, in a real sense, for our sakes:
we have to be shielded from the blinding glory
that is God until we have been sufficiently purged
of our sins to enable us to bear the blinding glory
of God's holiness.

But we cannot be forever speechless. We need to
and must talk about this glorious mystery. God
as the Godhead is forever love, and love is for
outpouring, self-donation. God has revealed that
God *is* love, God *was* love and God *will be* love
for ever and ever.

If God is love, what did God love from eternity?
There were those who said God must have loved
creation, which meant that creation was as eternal
as God. But we know from scripture that creation
is not co-eternal with God. Creation by its very

definition was brought into existence, so that there was when time was not. But, even if that were not so – even if creation was truly co-eternal with God – it would have been a thoroughly inadequate object for the divine love.

In the doctrine of the Trinity, God has deigned to reveal the secrets of the divine life and love. God is love from all eternity in a dynamic exchange of love and self-emptying: God the Father pours out all of the loving of the Father to an Object that is co-equal and co-eternal and, therefore, thoroughly adequate as an object of that divine love, with the capacity to receive that outpouring of the divine kenosis, of the divine self-emptying; and the Son, co-equal and co-eternal with the Father, returns that eternally outpoured love in equal measure, and the love that flows between them is God the Holy Spirit. God needed nothing outside of the godhead in order to be God.

God did not need us. What a glorious, what a fantastic verity to rejoice over: God *wanted* us in a very real sense. God was, and is, totally self-sufficient, and needed and needs nothing outside God in order to be God. God created us, God created the world from an amazing outpouring of the divine love.

The human mother will often 'need' a baby, perhaps as – in very traditional societies – the justification for her marriage. But, most frequently, mother and father *want* a baby and, even if the infant is delicate and requires constant medical care and demands all of the mother's time, it really is wonderful to behold just how utterly self-giving the mother almost always is. She nourished the foetus, which would not have been able to develop without the nourishing in the womb, entirely dependent on its mother, and it is quite amazing to watch.

She might have had a difficult pregnancy, requiring the constant attention of her obstetrician, but I have never come across a mother who resented her infant because of all the trouble she experienced during the pregnancy. Almost everywhere in the world, a mother who did resent her infant would be regarded as an aberration.

Every mother experiences some physical anguish at childbirth, and yet, when the baby emerges and is placed in her hands, she seems miraculously to forget all that pain and discomfort as she beholds her child at her breast, suckling away for all it is worth. I think, as I have said, that that is probably the best image of the divine love – loving through self-donation, from the beginning of the baby's life to its very end.

Again, there will be odd exceptions where a mother resents her child, perhaps because she knows she cannot handle the many children she has had to raise and nurture. But, most frequently, the image of the self-giving and doting mother is the closest depiction of God's love for us. The mother passionately loves this bundle of life, which has not earned it. How could a baby earn anything when it is as yet unable to do anything for itself – let alone doing anything for anyone else? The baby is totally dependent on its mother for everything. She feeds and bathes the baby, potty-trains it, sees to it that the baby has gorgeous baby attire and toys, even when the baby cannot as yet use them. The mother lavishes all her love on this bundle of joy, really expecting nothing in return.

God used the image of a mother to try to

describe the wonders of the divine love. God's people, Israel, had complained that God had abandoned them, that God had forgotten them. God's response was to ask, through the prophet: 'Can a mother forget the child she bore?'. It is a rhetorical question that expects the obvious answer that almost everybody would give – 'Of course not! There cannot be such an unnatural mother.' We know that mothers who have had to give up their children for adoption never forget those children, and sometimes they are reunited with them years later. But God goes on to say: 'Yes, it is highly unlikely that such an unnatural thing could happen – but, unlikely as it is, it just might happen. Well, Israel, I cannot and will not forget you – *your name is engraved on the palms of my hands*' (Isa. 49.14-16).

All the above has been an attempt to persuade us that God loves us, not *because* we are lovable, but rather that we are lovable only because God first loves us. And God wonderfully loves us, not because God needs us but because God wants us. As we have already observed, you don't say 'I want oxygen', as if it were a matter of some indifference. If you did not get it you would disintegrate into the nothing, the oblivion from which the divine fiat, the divine creative word, has brought us into being, into existence.

We have seen that God was God long before there was a world with human beings, and animals, and fish. All of this magnificent and teeming creation has come about through the outpouring love of the triune God, who lavishes the outpourings of the triune divine love as an act of sheer grace.

God loves you, God loves me, not because we could render to God what God lacked. God is fullness of being, needing nothing outside God in order for God to be God. God could have been God without us, without the rest of creation. But God decided otherwise. We were thus created as an act of divine grace, a free gift not to be earned – in fact, unearnable, because we were not there to give God the price of creating us.

Having been lavished with this gift, which is then followed by that other act of sheer grace, the self-giving of Jesus on the cross, all we are expected to do is to be thankful in accepting our freely given gift. God, who has created us in His image so that we are and can be God's viceroys, wants us to be as God to one another: caring, compassionate, loving and affirming of others, helping God to turn God's world into the paradise God wanted us to inhabit.

We who are freely loved and thus affirmed are meant to be as God to others, to seek to work for a world which has been preserved for the enjoyment of all. God longs that we, who are aware of our infinite worth, will see in one another the image of God and so recognize that each of us, whatever our gender, our sexual orientation or our nationality, are fundamentally members of one family: the human family. God's family is created to exist in a delicate network of interdependence, one on another, so that we actualize our complementarity, aware of our need of one another; so that we embody *ubuntu* – that I am because you are, and you are because I am; that indeed a person *is* a person only through other persons.

Then we would see a world where we did not end with so many nervous breakdowns, with so many stomach ulcers. We would live in a world where the rat-race would be obsolete. And we would have a world in which we did care for the environment, where we did not spend such obscene amounts of money on instruments of death and destruction.

We would evolve into a world where we cared for our environment as God's good creation. We would nurture what is left of the ozone layer. We would care enough to use other sources of energy – the sun, the wind, and water – and avoid the fossil fuels that are damaging that precious layer. We would be God's stewards, God's stand-ins, as those created in God's image, caring for one another truly as members of one family: the human family, God's family. Please, God, hasten that day before it is too late.

Topics for Discussion

- 'Stomach ulcers become status symbols as they are signs of just how hard one is working.' *Do you recognise this phenomenon? How might we help to break the cycle?*

- 'We find it extremely difficult to be comfortable with the ethos of grace – of sheer gift. It must certainly be very difficult for those who have never lacked for anything, who have not quite known what it is to be without, then to experience the exhilaration of being given – of being offered a gift.' *Why is it so much harder to receive than to give? Jesus said that it was 'easier for a camel to pass through the eye of a needle than for a rich man to enter the kingdom of heaven': why should this be so?*

6

In the Beginning, God; At the End, God

Irecall it as if it were yesterday when I heard those words, 'In the beginning, God; at the end, God', as the text of a sermon. The preacher was Father Trevor Huddleston CR, later Archbishop of the Province of the Indian Ocean and more widely known as the President of the International Anti-Apartheid Movement. It was on the eve of his departure from South Africa to return to the Mother House of the Community of the Resurrection in Mirfield, Yorkshire. His recall was a pre-emptive move on the part of his Superior, to forestall his being either arrested or deported. He had taken out South African citizenship, so the deportation option was not applicable in his case and his Community were fearful that he would be detained.

He had been a thorn in the side of the South African apartheid government, with his sharp critique of their abominable policies against those

who were not White in South Africa. He had
been a close friend of Oliver Tambo who left
the country to head up the African National
Congress (ANC) when it went into exile, and a
friend also of Nelson Mandela.

I don't recall any words of his sermon except
the text, and what follows is what I imagine he
would have said. It is to describe the depth of
his faith, which no machinations by politicians
would destroy. His last broadcast sermon, I
believe, would have been a piece of defiance,
putting the apartheid authorities on notice that,
even though they might seem invincible at
the time, their days were numbered. Evil and
injustice might be rampant then, but as sure
as anything they would one day have to give
account to the divine Judge, when they would
bite the dust.

It was a defiant last gesture. Whatever the
appearance to the contrary, they would get their
come-uppance, for God was not to be mocked.
Yes, it might not seem likely then, but one day
they would have to give account, as it were, of
their stewardship. God was the source of everything. Everything had its beginning with God,

and everything had its end, its consummation, its justification in the selfsame God. All would one day have to give account.

In the beginning, God; at the end, God. It is a tremendous text: that all emanates from this pre-existent one, who brought everything into being out of nothing, *ex nihilo*; who had nurtured and watched over the process of evolution until the emergence of *homo sapiens* – us. Until this point, creation as it were adored God by being what it was meant to be; from now on, the worship of God would be intentional and free. Of man and woman alone amongst God's creatures was it said that they had been created in the image of their Maker. As we have said previously, they were to be God's stand-ins, God's viceroys; to watch over, to tend and care for the rest of God's creation as God would have done, by being God's representatives. They were commanded to enjoy the wonders of this marvellous creation, to be fruitful and to multiply – as should creation also, that it should flourish, largely in order to provide for God's representatives, i.e. the man Adam and his spouse, Eve.

We have already seen how a relationship that should have been for flourishing and enjoyment and fulfilment went awry. Whatever we may call it, or however we may conceive of it and eventually describe it, something untoward happened. Where there should have been joy, now there was sadness; where there should have been flourishing, there was a blighted existence; where there should have been joyful fellowship, there was a leanness of spirit; where there should have been hope, there was despair; where there should have been teeming life, there was a cold, clammy death.

God had created humankind for fellowship with fellow human beings. Instead of that fellowship, there was a debilitating thinness of spirit. And the ground which should have produced in abundance what was needed to sustain God's human creatures and the gambolling, frisky animals had become a barren wilderness.

The Bible describes it all. Where human labour should have been productive, with the corn and the maize swaying in the gentle breezes, the earth now produced thistles and weeds. Instead of the lambs and the lions and the elephants, the birds and the bees, all frisky and playfully tugging at one another, it was all, as has been described so starkly, 'nature red in tooth and claw'. The peace and well-being that God had intended were lying torn and tattered in the bloodstained earth.

Now this is not a fanciful description. I visited Fort McMurray in the province of Alberta in Western Canada. I recall being taken on a tour by helicopter. It was a shocking experience to see what the landscape looked like, with puddles of oil floating on the river. I was told that, because of the tar sands, oil has been seeping naturally from down below and often into the rivers. Be that as it may, in previous years you did not have what is commonplace today in this area. The water in many parts is not potable; fish are dying, covered in horrific cancerous sores, and the First Nation people are bearing the brunt of all this degradation. They used to grow their own food. It is getting increasingly difficult to do so. They have depended on fishing from time immemorial, but now many fish are suffering and dying from cancer.

The traditional ways are becoming more and more impossible to sustain, and the people are being driven off the land into the cities, where many succumb to the urban way of life. They do not even cope at school, where they have a troubling dropout rate, so the shattering statistics about drug use, alcoholism, crime and imprisonment are not surprising. These things did not happen when they could live their lives following traditional ways. If the oil was seeping into the rivers, as is asserted, it certainly did not have the dire consequences that are evident today.

There can be no doubt at all that something serious is happening; that climate change is not just a theory thought up by scientists who have nothing better to do. We have not kept and nurtured nature as God had intended us to do. The ice cap is melting with devastating consequences. Polar bears are drowning because the ice is too thin to carry their weight. People living in the Arctic have seen staggering changes in their lifestyles. They can no longer visit one another easily, because skiing is hazardous when the ice may not be able to support their weight. That is what the Icelandic bishop told us in the church service I referred to earlier, in Tromso in Norway a few years ago, to mark World Environment

Day. In the same service, someone from the Pacific Islands described how the trees on her island home were dying because of the rising salt seawater level; a few islands have already disappeared under the sea. Carbon emissions are playing havoc with the ozone layer. Some say we have only a very few years left before the climate changes become irreversible.

God wanted us to live in a paradise, a garden which we would tend. Only those who are wilfully blind can say that climate change is for the birds, that it has not been shown to be something credible. Otherwise, we need to ask why we are seeing such unusual phenomena as, for example, the torrential rains that have devastated so many parts of the globe. What about the tsunamis? Or the exceptionally long winters/ summers with unusually extreme temperatures in so many different parts of the world?

I pray that we will come to our senses, and very quickly. If we do not urgently find substitutes for the fossil fuels we are using so recklessly then it will be curtains for us. This is the only planet home we have. None of us can say: 'Stop the world – I want to jump off', in order to find refuge elsewhere. We can only really survive together, just as, if we do not mend our ways, we will undoubtedly perish together.

Our attitude to the environment is a moral issue. For Christians, it is also a religious issue, because it was God who created all that is, and God instructed us to keep it and to till it.

God longed for us to be co-creators with God. We made a hash of things. We were meant to live in friendship and harmony with the rest of creation and with our fellow humans. Instead we can see what we have done – and what we continue to do – to nature. There is a dreadful scourge of poaching, when rare species are threatened with extinction. A far cry from the paradise God had intended.

Yes, creation is now horrendously red in tooth and claw: there are both animal and human predators, a far cry from the dream God had cherished. And so there was a fight to the death between Eve's descendants and those of the serpent. Eve's descendants would crush the serpent's head, and the serpent's descendants would bruise the human's heels.

God had longed for us to live in a paradise with friendly animals and a garden of plants that would have grown without too much back-breaking toil, with not too many weeds to be uprooted. God had hoped we would dwell in this paradise, aware that we were family, with a God who was not too far away – a God who could figuratively drop by of an afternoon for a chat with God's human creatures.

Praying and worshipping would not have been, as is so often the case, a drudgery. Praying would have been a matter of course, like two friends conversing without the bane of often debilitating distractions. Whatever it was that happened, it made communion with the Creator so often a draining slog.

Whatever we may think of those stories of the beginning times, most of us will admit that they depict what many of us experience daily. We are aware that we know Paradise Lost. God had wanted us to be as a family. Tragically, God's intention was frustrated: brother turned on brother and so Cain murdered Abel, a fratricide that has been echoed too many times. Nazi Germans turned on fellow Germans who happened to be Jews, and the result was the Holocaust. Very recently, one million Tutsis were assassinated by their Hutu fellow-Rwandans. The members of Boko Haram are Nigerians. They have turned viciously on fellow-Nigerians, their most horrendous atrocity being the abduction of over 200 schoolgirls, forcing them to become Muslims and selling them off as child brides for only $12.

The catalogue is endless and ghastly. And this is an account of only a very few of the atrocities being perpetrated today. It would be devastating if we described the blood-letting that has happened since *homo sapiens* appeared on the scene, God's dream lying in tatters.

God has not given up on God's dream. It has been kept alive by those whom God has sent to remind us of it. Just as Martin Luther King Jr famously proclaimed 'I have a dream' in a deeply moving address in Washington DC, so God can keep reminding us, 'I have a dream that one day my people will know that I created them to be a family; I created them for togetherness; I created them for complementarity; I created them for a delicate network of interdependence where each makes up for what is lacking in the other'.

Isaiah proclaimed that God had not given up on God's dream, that all God's creation would be one of peace, where everything co-existed in harmony and peace. This coming time would be like the beginning time depicted in those early chapters of Genesis.

Isaiah describes such a time, and in his description there seems to have been a deliberate intention to nullify the Genesis story of Adam and Eve. The child can play over the serpent's hole unscathed. In the fallen world, lambs would normally be a delicious meal for the lion, but in Isaiah's imagery they lie peacefully together as God had seemed to intend in the time of the beginning (Isa. 11.1–16). To describe this phenomenon, the Germans said *'Endzeit ist Urzeit'*: the time of the end is as the time of the beginning.

Elsewhere the prophet Isaiah, echoed in identical words by the prophet Micah, speaks of a time of universal peace, when we will 'beat our swords into pruning-hooks', and all humankind will march to the Holy City to be, once again, one community living in peace and harmony (Isa. 2.4).

This dream became more and more remote as the Chosen People reneged and did not honour the compact they had entered into with God on Mount Sinai, after their escape from bondage in Egypt. The canonical prophets became aware of this process, and Deutero-Isaiah came to the point where he saw the remnant as just one representative figure: the Suffering Servant.

To many, this individual was repulsive and unattractive and so they rejected him. But, in the divine economy, it was he who would attain the redemption of God's people through his vicarious suffering. So Israel ended up being one person. He was tempted as we are tempted, but he did not succumb and remained sinless. For us, he experienced the extreme form of alienation and separation from God: death. Wonderfully, He rose again, ascended to heaven and now reigns forever with the Father and the Holy Spirit, worshipped and adored by the whole company of heaven forever and forever.

When Jesus became our Saviour and was born of the Virgin Mary His mother, He assumed our human nature and so, for instance, He was really tempted as we are – it was no charade. He could have failed and succumbed to temptation. He resisted the Devil throughout his life until his final triumph on the Cross, for the Devil, as we know, had tempted Him in the garden of Gethsemane to escape the cup of suffering.

He triumphed even unto death and, before giving up the ghost, could shout triumphantly: 'It is finished!', far better translated, not as if it were a whimper – 'I'm done for' – but rather: 'I have accomplished it; I have triumphed; I have brought things to their proper fulfilment'.

That is why it was an appropriate symbol that the curtain in the Temple, which separated the holy place where normal services were held from the Holy of Holies which housed the Ark of the Covenant and was entered only by the High Priest (and that only once a year, on the Day of Atonement), was torn from top to bottom. Now we could have direct access to God, at any time, always.

We had no reason, we have no reason now, to want to hide from God, as Adam and Eve had done. In fact, far from hiding from God we are wonderfully already in the heaven of heavens, for we in our baptism have been grafted into Christ; we have been already united with Christ by baptism.

We have been crucified and buried with Him, and have already risen with Him in His resurrection; and, wonder of wonders, we have already ascended with Him, and even now you and I – yes – reign with Him at the right hand of the Father, worshipped and adored by the whole host of heaven; by the four living creatures, by the angels and archangels, the cherubim and the seraphim as well as the 24 elders (perhaps 12 each for the old Israel and the new Israel).

The four living creatures do not cease to worship, but if they should then the 24 elders descend from their thrones, doffing their golden crowns, and worship Him who sits on the throne. The four living creatures cry out day and night (though we are to learn that there is no night, there is no sun, nor moon nor stars – there is no need of them because the glory of the crucified, ascended and glorified Son of God provides the abiding illumination).

We must not be literalistic. The book of the Revelation of St John is hugely imaginative.

No one has experienced what the author was describing, and yet he did succeed in helping us to catch a glimpse of, and be caught up in, the liturgy of heaven. No one has returned to give a description of what heaven would be like.

We do not really know what it is not to be spatiotemporally conditioned. We do not know what it must be like. What we read in the book of Revelation are pointers, adumbrations. There are what seem, if we are dull and literal-minded, to be glaring contradictions. At one place the author says that the 24 elders are sitting on their thrones; at another, we are told of the selfsame elders that, each time the four living creatures cease to worship God, the elders descend their thrones and worship – but then we hear that the many creatures worship God ceaselessly, so when do the elders get a chance to worship?

My New Testament professor at King's College, London, Christopher Evans, used to say, 'Revelation should really be set to music for us to fathom its verities', and you realize what a splendid suggestion that is when you have listened to the worship of heaven interpreted by, say, Handel in *The Messiah* – 'Worthy is the

Lamb' or the Hallelujah Chorus, which leave one almost breathless. The redeemed – all of us – now inhabit not a garden but a city, which is a perfect cube, with streets paved with gold, built on the foundations of the Apostles, echoing the Epistle to the Ephesians (Eph. 2.19ff.).

The history of the world has been a sorry tale of wars, deceit, alienations, injustice and oppression and godlessness but, in the consummation of all things, all of these are reversed – for Jesus the Lamb of God without blemish has ransomed us for God from all peoples and nations and founded a new community and fellowship (Rev 5.14; Rev 7). The redeemed, the 144,000 who are sealed, are multiples of the old people of God, those who had been unfaithful and disobedient. The new people of God have been faithful and obedient.

* * *

Conclusion

In the beginning, God; at the end, God. As a small aside, I do not think that the God who risked the loss of 99 well-behaved sheep to go after the obstreperous, troublesome old ram that had gone astray and, when he found it with tattered and torn fleece, carried it home on his shoulders, would be the God of a heavenly company that would gloat over the damned.

I think that the blessed will mourn for those who finally reject God's invitation but, as I have already shared, I align myself with Origen, who in his universalism taught that ultimately even Satan would be converted, because even he would not be able to resist the attraction of the divine love; and then God would truly be all in all. And the times of the End would be as the times of the Beginning – *Endzeit ist Urzeit*, Amen. To God be the glory, Amen, Amen.

In the beginning, God; at the end – God.

Topics for Discussion

- 'Praying and worshipping would not have been, as is so often the case, a drudgery. Praying would have been a matter of course, like two friends conversing without the bane of often debilitating distractions. Whatever it was that happened, it made communion with

117

the Creator so often a draining slog.' *Why does prayer sometimes seem like a drudgery? How can we open up our channels of communication with the Creator?*

- 'The Germans said "*Endzeit ist Urzeit*": the time of the end is as the time of the beginning.' *The poet T. S. Eliot wrote, 'In my end is my beginning'. What does this mean? How can it be true?*

PART TWO

Desmond Tutu was the first black Archbishop of Cape Town (1986–1996), and President of the All Africa Conference of Churches (1987–1997). Born in South Africa in 1931, he trained originally as a teacher before being ordained priest in 1961. He was awarded the Nobel Peace Prize in 1984 and two years later was the first recipient of the Albert Schweitzer Prize for Humanitarianism, an award to those 'who have made exemplary contributions to humanity and the environment'. These awards helped to establish the global profile of the struggle against apartheid, a system which Tutu vigorously and publicly opposed whilst consistently advocating non-violent protest and reconciliation between all the parties. Other awards include the Gandhi Peace Prize (2007) and the Presidential Medal of Freedom (2009).

When, in 1994, South Africa elected Nelson Mandela as its first black President, Desmond Tutu was given the honour of introducing the new President to the nation. Mandela subsequently appointed Tutu to chair the Truth and Reconciliation Commission, set up to investigate and report on the atrocities committed by both sides under apartheid.

Tutu has been publicly critical of South Africa's ANC government and has continued to speak out on behalf of the poor and powerless, not only in South Africa but throughout the world, despite having formally retired from public life on reaching the age of 80. His friend Nelson Mandela said of him, 'Desmond Tutu's voice will always be the voice of the voiceless.'

* * *

In the summer of 2014, in an interview recorded in London, he looked back on his life and reflected on his Christian faith and the spiritual influences that have helped to shape him.

'ARCH' IN CONVERSATION: A SPIRITUAL RETROSPECTIVE

I wanted to start by asking you about earliest memories and expectations, and how you first came to believe...

When I became aware of myself, I was already a believer in the sense that if you had Christian parents you were baptized, and so they'd made that decision for you. On the whole, one had the fairly standard views about God: a grandfather, somewhere up in the sky, who is generally well-disposed but if you are naughty then be careful – you might end up in the warm place! I remember visiting quite a number of homes that had these very lurid pictures of hell with people who'd been enjoying themselves being taken down into the fire, and then a sedate white-clad procession going up to heaven. You didn't wonder why it was that the guys who were enjoying themselves were in the Devil's fire and the ones who were the sourpusses were going up to heaven.

I'd been taught to say prayers before I retired – fairly standard prayers, maybe just the Lord's Prayer and then jumping into bed, but it's still something... When I was maybe seven or so I did have what, looking back, was a kind of vision in which the Devil was trying to pull me – again, those standard pictures of the Devil with his tail and horns – and this is the first time that I've spoken of this... I had a clear understanding that someone remonstrated with the Devil and someone said – God said – 'This is my child'. But that disappeared and I never told anyone about it.

We started out as Methodists. I was baptized in the Methodist Church as an infant and followed my father, who was a headmaster. We were very peripatetic – here one time, then moved to some other locality – but we were in the Methodist Church. When my older sister (she's still alive) became very friendly with the daughter of an AME pastor, I became a member of that church (African Methodist Episcopal Church: it's a Black church that came from the United States; episcopal – with bishops. Very beautiful singing). Then my sister went to an Anglican (boarding) high school where the Community of the Resurrection (CR) and all of those people

126

were involved, and she said she wanted to be confirmed as an Anglican. My parents said yes that was OK, and we all duly followed her into the Anglican Church.

Who were the most significant spiritual influences on you?

As I grow older, I'm so aware of all the people who influenced me for the good – really, that's why it's such a silly thing when anyone speaks about the 'self-made' person – and I am so deeply thankful. I am aware of just how incredibly blessed I was in the first Anglican priest that I met, a black priest in Ventersdorp where I grew up: Father Zachariah Sekgaphane. What struck me about him (although almost certainly this is a very idealized picture) was that I never once saw him angry.

The second thing that had a particular impact on me was that we were servers and, as well as the main church, he had satellite churches, usually on farms, where we servers accompanied him. The people would be dancing attention on him; they'd have prepared a sumptuous meal for him in one of the rondavels and then we lesser mortals would be going to eat somewhere outside. My clear, lasting memory is that Fr Sekgaphane never went to sit down for his meal before ensuring that we lesser mortals had in fact been fed. That was something that remained with me; he had this remarkable charm, and I am so grateful that he was one of the people who touched my life.

Then there was Trevor Huddleston. My mother was a cook at a hostel for blind black women at an institute called Ezenzeleni, where you do things for yourself (that's what *Ezenzeleni* means – the place where you do things for yourselves, you help yourselves). It was started by an extraordinary British couple, the Reverend Arthur Blaxall and his wife, Florence – they founded two institutes for the blind, one in Cape Town and this one. Es'kia Mphahlele, who later wrote *Down Second Avenue*, was a high school teacher at Orlando High School in Soweto but resigned; he left teaching and came to work at Ezenzeleni as a driver/clerk, and he tried to teach me boxing. We used to go for a run every Saturday morning.

You paid for education – at high school, it wasn't very high fees but you had to buy your own books; and then for a little while there was free government feeding, even in high school. To begin with, that was only for white pupils – pupils who didn't need it – and they used to throw most of it away. I was the only black boy with his own bicycle, which my father had bought me, and I used to go and buy newspapers and things. I remember that one day I saw black kids scavenging in the dustbins and they were getting perfectly OK apples and sandwiches and so on, because the white kids preferred the lunches that their mothers had prepared. We who needed it were not getting it and, when we did get it, Prime Minister Verwoerd then stopped it, because he said 'If we can't feed all of these black children then we shouldn't feed some.' Imagine if people had said 'We won't treat this TB patient because we can't cure them all'...

So at this early age you were intensely aware of (the evil that became) *apartheid and that it was an evil?*

We were aware of it, of course; of the disparity between black and white. When we were in Standards 5 and 6 we used to read a history textbook written by a Methodist minister called Whitehead, who had been a missionary. It

129

claimed that David Livingstone had 'discovered' the Victoria Falls. Now, you 'discover' something where there are no people; here is David Livingstone, who 'discovers' the Victoria Falls, and then these Blacks who were sitting there, they say 'Oh yes, now we see'. So the fact that this thing had been there all the time and that they had seen it simply didn't count – the Whites were always 'discovering' things, because we were just nonentities, we were nothing.

Did you think that this was how it was going to be for the rest of your life? Did you hope that things might ever change?

We hoped that things would change, but we were certainly not as politically aware as the world we are commemorating today – June 16 (the Soweto Uprising), and all of those who have come after. My father wasn't a member of a union, for example: it would not have been allowed. Black trade unions were not recognized; if they existed they were not acknowledged as an organization.

You mentioned Trevor Huddleston...

I must have been eight or nine when I was standing with my mother as a white priest in a long cassock and a big hat swept past, and he doffed his hat to my mother. (Although John Allen says the dates are not quite right and it may have been Father Raymond Raynes, I always thought it was Trevor.) But a white man doffing his hat to a black woman, in South Africa? That really shook me.

But it was in 1945 that I met Trevor Huddleston for the first time – well, I didn't meet him: it was VE Day, and he had come to address the school about the victory of the Allies. We were all fascinated by how he pronounced 'Nazi' – we used to say 'Nazzy' and he said 'Nartsi', so we were laughing at him a little bit, thinking that this was very peculiar.

At the time I was travelling daily to and from the high school by train, but I think it was at the end of Form 2 that I discovered that the Community of the Resurrection had set up a hostel in Sophiatown – 74, Meyer Street – for students and young men who were working and did not have accommodation. That would save on money and travel, so I went to live with the Community (or at least to live in the hostel). There were about 30 or 40 of us, and the priory was next door with this fantastic place, Christ the King Church. That was when we got to know Trevor.

One day, he had been away – usually, when he returned we would go and welcome him, but this time I didn't go to meet him. I had a splitting headache and I told the others to say Welcome Back for me. One of the Fathers came and took my temperature; I think my temperature was high, so they took me to Coronation Hospital and I ended up in hospital for a month. (There were hardly any black doctors; the doctors were white, but the nurses were black, and I fell for one of them. If she came to take my pulse and temperature they were quite wrong, I'm sure!)

They discovered that I had TB, and I was transferred to the isolation hospital, and that was when my relationship with Trevor grew. He was a very busy person. If he was not with us or in his office then he was with, maybe, Harry Oppenheimer*; he was meeting with top people, and I was very struck by the fact that he was so regular in visiting me. As a township urchin I was thinking, A white man caring for a black kid in this fashion? He was an enormous, enormous influence on me. I know it wasn't just on me – when you see Walter (*later Archbishop*) Makhulu and the other people who came through; the CR actually were a fantastic organization.

Years later, at the Lambeth Conference in 1988 when we were all of us archbishops, Trevor told me something I'd not known. He said that, on one of his visits to me, the doctor called him aside and said 'Your young friend is not going to make it.' I think I know when this was, because there was a time when I started coughing up blood – on a general ward, you could see that anyone who started coughing up blood would be wheeled out to the mortuary.

I remember when this started; I remember one morning going to the bathroom and this thing

* South African politician and businessman, one of the world's richest men, well known for his opposition to apartheid.

was coming in floods, well I said to God, 'God, if it means I've got to die – OK. Of course I want to live, but if it is that I'm going to die then OK.' I cannot describe to you the peace that came over me after I had made that particular decision. And actually, after a little while, this whole thing subsided and then ended, but I do remember getting to the point where I was accepting of that particular outcome.

Trevor gave me my first copy of a very thin, pocket New Testament; and I read *Cry, the Beloved Country* in manuscript because Alan Paton was a very close friend of Trevor, and at the time he was Warden of Diepkloof Reformatory in Soweto. Trevor let me read that, and then it became a bestseller all over the world – those were some of the incredible privileges that we had. But the most important thing, in relation to what was coming after – I think for most of us who were involved with CR, was getting to know that there are white people who care for us, who really care for us. I think that was why there was far less bloodshed against the Whites, because it meant that our people weren't anti-White, they were anti-apartheid; and of course the Communists also helped in that they were almost all white people who accepted Blacks on genuinely equal terms. I do believe that that relationship with Trevor certainly saved me, and many others who had fairly similar relationships, from anti-Whiteism.

And then, of course, going to theological college. For a very long time, from an early age, I wanted to be a doctor and then, after I'd contracted TB, I was even more determined – I wanted to find a cure for this. I was admitted to medical school but, because we didn't have the where-withal for the fees, I left. I followed my father and became a teacher; I enjoyed teaching. My older sister was also a teacher, and my wife Leah was a teacher too, but when Bantu Education was introduced we said 'No, we don't want to be collaborating with this travesty.' So we both decided to resign our posts and she went off to train as a nurse. I eventually found my way to St Peter's Theological College where I began training to be a priest. I can't pretend I went to train for the priesthood from noble motives, or an overwhelming sense of vocation – I had very few other options! So perhaps that's one of God's little jokes.

When I was at theological college, I met most of the CR again – they had one or two black members, but most of them were white. One of them, who was vice-principal of the college when I came, was Timothy Stanton, whose twin sister Hannah had been detained and then deported. He was very much quieter, but he too got arrested because he refused to testify against someone else who'd been arrested, and he served, I think, five months in jail.

When you were speaking about Fr Sekgaphane, you said how much you admired the fact that you never saw him angry. Is there a place for anger? Even a duty to be angry in the face of injustice?

I do think that anger has a place so long as it isn't in response to a slight to you personally. If there is anger because of what has been done to others, then that is justifiable. If you do not wish the worst to befall whoever provoked the anger, if you want and you hope that that person can change, you give them options – you always have to hope they will change.

Hope, as you know, is not the same thing as optimism; hope is a far deeper thing, and it does not depend on the superficial. It is the same principle that brings good out of the most ghastly thing, a crucifixion: hope that out of that crucifixion can come the victory of the resurrection, which is a victory that says 'I, when I am lifted up, will draw all to myself'.

That is fundamental to my faith; that, yes, this God is constantly amazing in the fact that God wants us to be persons not automatons. We are persons, we have the freedom to choose and a God who says I'd much rather you went to hell freely than compel you to come to heaven. As I've said before, I agree entirely with Origen when he says that the Devil is going to find the love of God totally irresistible, so that, in the end, the Devil is going to be drawn back, because I could not myself square a God where the saints were, as it were, gloating.

You were talking beautifully about the nature of Christian hope – how do you respond to the Dalai Lama's suggestion that 'the object of human life is to be happy'?

Knowing him, I would say that he didn't intend that to mean happy-clappy. He's been in exile for more than 50 years and, when you meet him, where you are expecting that you would be finding someone gnarled and bitter and angry, he is so full of fun and compassion.

I would myself say that an exegesis of that would be, What is fullness of life? When we are what God intends us to be, of course we will be happy, but happy how? You discover, in fact, that it is when you are intent on making others happy that in the process happiness steals up on you, it comes like a thief in the night. When you go out looking for it, it evaporates and disappears, and so I would say Yes, isn't it after all our hope that we will share in the eternal bliss of God? But as to how we get to be happy – well, I can't say that we now have a right to that; it's in the gift of God, and it involves enjoying the joy of God.

In relation to Lent, for some of us the vision of God is something painful – that's probably why I resist the Dalai Lama's suggestion about happiness, because of suffering. But he has himself suffered, as you so rightly say...

I think in part Lent is to acknowledge that the way things are is not what God intended. The

Bible after all says God wanted us to inhabit a paradise – the intention of God was that we would flourish in our humanity, precisely because we were not turned inwards. That is why God can say, even though Adam had the animals and the trees and things, It is not good for him to be alone – you can't find fulfilment in yourself. Your fulfilment is always – I've experienced it, sometimes it was very fleeting, but some of our best moments have been when we gave; when we sought to be caring of another and were not looking for any rewards. I remember especially – when your kids were younger, when you came in and you brought them, say, a toy, their joy doubled up your joy. When we have become, unwittingly perhaps, what God intended us to be, we do experience something that you can get in no other way. You can't counterfeit it. We are caught, as it were; made happy by surprise. Surprised by happiness – by joy.

When you have seen a mother who maybe during the day has had a very demanding job: that mother, if her child is unwell, thinks nothing of sitting the whole night through by the bed of her child. It's an extraordinary thing and it is wonderful to discover that God has regarded mother love as about the highest form of human emotion. When the people of Israel say to God 'You have forgotten us', God says 'What? do you think a mother can forget the child she bore?' And he's asking that question expecting the answer 'Of course not!'

Then God says this totally unlikely thing, this unnatural thing – we assert so confidently, all of us, that no mother that we know could forget the child she bore. And God says Yes, but this unlikely thing just might happen. Supposing, as often happened, when a girl child is pregnant out of wedlock and the family are agitated and they want as quickly as possible to have the child adopted, trying their damnedest to have their daughter forget. Now it just is possible that, because this whole thing is so traumatic, she might – so this thing just could possibly happen; but God says, 'I will not forget you *because your name is engraved on the palm of my hand.*'

When He was tempted in the desert, Jesus knew despair and failure which are common conditions: how do we overcome that?

It is so important for us to realize that our Lord's humanity was not a fake; it was for real, it was

140

authentic. God did not whisper to him privately
to say 'Oh don't worry, it will be OK.'

It's quite amazing, it really is staggering when
you come to think of what it meant for Our Lord
to say 'I give up', or, as Philippians tells you,
'emptying himself' (Phil. 2.7); and he didn't have
a private little button that he could press when
things were tough to bring in the divinity. He
got thoroughly clobbered as a human being, and
I suppose as you grow older you realize just how
extraordinary that is. He was tempted as we are,
except that he was without sin.

What have been the disappointments in your own life?

In my own life, I would say I got shook up and
really disappointed when they said I'd failed
Standard 6 – I was quite clear I hadn't and thank-
fully my father also believed that. I wouldn't have
been able to repeat the class, and my father went
and talked to the principal of a high school and
they took me on, and fortunately I came out
first in the class, after having been told I had not
passed Standard 6, so for what was the first year
of high school I did quite well. But I remember

I couldn't sleep that night when the results came and I had failed; I was crying the whole night through, and actually that was when I realized, I think, that up to that point I was cocky and depended on myself.

I was about 12 or 13 and I had been promoted early: I spent only three months in Standard 5 before they promoted me to Standard 6, which was the last year. They all reckoned I was going to do very well (I thought I was going to do very well, too!), and this – I was brought down several pegs. It made me start to realize that I was not all-conquering and all-knowing, and that was when I began being able to say, 'If it be your will...'

What about disappointments in South Africa today? With the fall of apartheid, you must have dreamed of a wonderful new world, and it hasn't happened.

There is still terrible poverty, and water is polluted, but one is still incredibly thankful and exhilarated by the fact of being free. You know, it's not easy to describe to someone who hasn't shared that experience: that today, in my country, I don't have to carry a pass. When I see a police officer I don't have to be scared, I don't have to pat myself to be sure that I do have my pass on me. I can live anywhere that I can afford; our children can go now to any school – including private schools, if you are able to afford them.

The first black leaders of South Africa – Oliver Tambo, for example, was a teacher and then became a lawyer, and he had Mandela as a clerk. Most people in that generation, almost all of them, would have been people who were educated because a mother, a grandmother was doing washing or laundry for some white people. They were actually remarkable, because they were paid so little; I remember my mother would work a whole day for a white woman and get two shillings for her pay, and my parents thought that that was not bad. And yet she had also got to find the fare or walk the distance to her place of work and back...

If you look at most of the people who qualified then, they would have been people who, many of them, would have been studying privately; and to think that we did have people qualifying as doctors, for example, given those circumstances

– it's quite, quite amazing, and maybe we have lost something in the entitlement mentality, where people think something is due to them. In a way, yes, of course it should be the case that if you have the capacity, if you have the skill, the ability, you ought to be able to get on; but I think many of our kids are going to miss out, because so many things are now falling into their laps that they do not have the same kind of appreciation that my generation has, and so our country is at an interesting place.

One very important recommendation from the Truth and Reconciliation Commission was the one about the Wealth Tax – if that had been implemented, we would not have eradicated poverty, but the gap would have been much narrower. In fact the government accepted hardly any of the important recommendations that were made. We said that people should be given reparation over six years – it was a piffling amount, but it was making a statement. They didn't accept that, and some of the people died before they received anything, and even when they did get anything it was a one-off amount of 30,000 rand.

Your book suggests that, although the world is very very complicated, the central message of the Gospel is very, very simple – deceptively so. Have you always felt that way?

No! When I was teaching at Emory University in Atlanta, I told the students that I really just have one sermon to preach, one lecture to give. At the end of our time together, two or three years, they gave me a plaque which was – they didn't say 'Nobel', they said 'This is the Noble Award for preaching, even if it is preaching only one sermon, because in fact the one sermon that each one of us needs to know is that God loves you.'

God loves you. That's the sum total of it, and nothing, absolutely nothing can change that fact. It is when we begin to realize that truth that we then try to live it, not in order to impress God into loving us but to say to God 'Thank you for loving me.' Trevor used to quote Julian of Norwich, which I was re-reading this morning, where she says, God never STARTED to love us; and there are those strange things in the Epistle and Jeremiah: 'Before I formed you in the womb, I knew you' (Jer. 1.5), and I found

another, almost similar in Isaiah. In one of the
Servant Songs, Isaiah says 'God loved me before
he formed me' (Isa. 49.1) – something like that;
and you think of Ephesians saying also *God chose
us in Christ before the foundations of the world*. I
don't think that we have grasped that.

It is simple, but it's not easy. It's not easy to
understand... It makes us realize that God's
standards are low, because there's nothing I can
do that is going to make God say Pah! and spit
us out – that is what I would tell the students.
I would say, when you think about the Trinity –
yes, God is love, and what did God love before
God created us? And there were those who said
creation is as eternal as God, but you realize
that in fact creation would be an inadequate
object for the divine love. And then you realize
that the doctrine of the Trinity is a fantastic
doctrine in that it says that within the Godhead
there is this dynamic movement – that God
is a kenotic God, a self-emptying god. God is
forever pouring out all of God's love, and the
object of this love has to be co-equal, co-eternal
with the subject, and also to return this love in
equal measure.

And so you come to realize that our worth is incredible – you see, God did not need us; God does not need anything outside of God to be God, so we are like the child of a marriage who is longed-for and wanted, rather than needed. God says, 'Yes, I *want* you' – you are not a divine afterthought.

What is the message of Easter in all this?

God, in seeking to demonstrate the love that this God has for us, says 'I will live as one of you', so God comes down; God knows from the inside what it is to be tempted, and knows the strength of temptation, because God has experienced it but does not in fact give in. The person who knows us, and who knows how tough it is to get to the top of the mountain, is the one who gets there when all the others fall by the wayside, but this God who is willing to be like us at the lowest point also promises that we will reach the highest point.

Now, how can we speak about the fact that he dies and rises again, and you and I have also died, have risen, have ascended and are in heaven with this Jesus? He didn't take a shortcut – he didn't have a first-class ticket. When we look at our world, in reality there is no hope for it; in human terms, we are rushing to hell. If you doubt it, look around you: at Syria, at Ukraine, Iraq, at South Sudan and the Central African Republic; look at the number of people who have been killed in Kenya because they couldn't speak Somali and they were not Muslim. How can President Assad justify gassing children, the children of his own citizens?

A God who is prepared to leave 99 sheep to go and look for one is a God who refuses to give up, and God says 'I am not going to undo what I did. They are human beings, they are moral agents and I gave them the freedom to be able to choose. I am not going to nullify that gift, and the only way we can reverse what is happening is by getting as many as possible to emulate this Son of mine who lived a human life, who was hungry, who was afraid, who knew despair; who knew the whole gamut of being human, and was able to be obedient even unto death'. There have been those who have walked that path – those we know, like St Francis, and the many that we don't know.

God refuses to give up, and we who are enlisted to be fellow-workers with God know that the only reason we continue is that Death did not have the last word; that Good Friday was not the end of the story. The story culminates on Easter Day, so for ever we know that good WILL prevail. We know that you can have a Bonhoeffer, or any of these incredible human beings who show us glimpses of the divine – and that is Easter.

ACKNOWLEDGMENTS

I am honoured to have been asked to write the Archbishop of Canterbury's Lent Book for 2015. I realize just how unworthy I am for such a high distinction and was quite shocked that I could be asked.

Thank you, Your Grace; thank you for the help that the Rev. Dr Jo Wells, the Archbishop's Chaplain, provided. I am deeply indebted to Robin Baird-Smith for his enormous patience with a somewhat recalcitrant author. I have been given a free hand with help always available. I want to express my gratitude also to dear Lynn Franklin, my hugely supportive and caring agent, and her colleagues. I would not have met the deadline without the help of my PA, Vivian Ford and her colleagues Razaan Bailey and Mthunzi Gxashe. Poor dears, my hieroglyphics must have driven them round the bend.

Thank you all.

+DT